Beside
the
Rio Hondo

Beside
The
Rio Hondo

A Memoir of Rural New Mexico

Phaedra Greenwood

SUNSTONE
PRESS

SANTA FE

Book and cover design by Vicki Ahl

Sunstone books may be purchased for educational, business, or sales promotional use. For information please write: Special Markets Department, Sunstone Press, P.O. Box 2321, Santa Fe, New Mexico 87504-2321.

Library of Congress Cataloging-in-Publication Data:

Greenwood, Phaedra, 1942-
Beside the Rio Hondo : a memoir of rural New Mexico / by Phaedra Greenwood.
    p. cm.
 ISBN 978-0-86534-518-8 (softcover : alk. paper)
 1. Greenwood, Phaedra, 1942- 2. Journalists--United States--Biography.
3. Journalists--New Mexico--Biography. I. Title.

PN4874.G699A3 2008
070.92--dc22
[B]
                                    2007040956

WWW.SUNSTONEPRESS.COM
SUNSTONE PRESS / POST OFFICE BOX 2321 / SANTA FE, NM 87504-2321 /USA
(505) 988-4418 / ORDERS ONLY (800) 243-5644 / FAX (505) 988-1025

For Sara, Alexander and Jim

Contents

Foreword

*P*haedra Greenwood's *Beside the Rio Hondo* evokes in earthy detail the hardships and miracles of everyday life during her years of living alone in a sparsely settled Hispano community in Northern New Mexico, surrounded by mountains that have been considered sacred by the Taos Pueblo Indians for a thousand years. Through her loving sense of place and her sacred view of nature there glows a kind of recognizable glory, the feelings and meanings that permeate her personal life. Her memoir is the story of how, in a lonely struggle against social, psychological, and economic odds, she re-establishes her home and a sense of belonging to the land. First comes the slow letting go of the past, the ardent striving for a balanced life, and finally, the joyous grounding of self in the habit of nurturing and loving. In the end, she becomes "solid and rooted in who I am—a woman who stands by herself . . . married heart and soul to the fierce and vibrant spirit of this land."

Like the rushing silver river itself, *Beside the Rio Hondo* is a source of comfort and revitalization for all of us who, anxious about the encroachment of machines in the planetary as well as the American garden, seek a path to higher consciousness, to emerge out of our own canyons of solitude.

Greenwood passionately opposes untoward forms of

restraint and confinement. Not simply a feminist outcry, but a defining characteristic of literature of the American West, this opposition leads her, a devoted mother and competent Jill-of-all-trades, to part ways with her husband, Aaron, and exchange security for authenticity. Paradoxically, the growth in awareness of the wholeness and fullness of life seems to depend upon silence and enclosure by the land, which reveal for her the road to liberation.

"I want to go on no matter what comes next. It begins to feel like freedom. I feel centered in a new and more constant way by what I have voluntarily given up. Something else comes to fill the void and sustain me.

"I can bear pain and loss; what I can't bear is being imprisoned. My heart feels as if it is opening and opening, and as it does, I get lighter and lighter. The grief and tears are mingled with the joy, the anger with the love. If I love and have nothing at stake, no one can ever take my life away from me. I am prepared to be a wanderer in the world just as much as I am prepared to live quietly at home alone."

Having come from a family of wanderers and literary dreamers, Greenwood, herself determined to be a writer, knows she has the passion, the resilience, and the resourcefulness she needs for the job. But if Aaron sells the house that is her home and cuts her adrift, the writing will become even more difficult. What makes *Beside the Rio Hondo* a particularly compelling narrative, a profoundly American one, is the tension between the security of home and the possibility of displacement.

When Henry James chose to live in England because "the skinniness and aridity of America," as his brother William called it, somehow failed to yield up material for fiction, he anticipated an attitude prevalent in the East today, namely that the West is a cultural backwater. The blank area between New York and Hollywood must be paved, poisoned, and overpopulated before it qualifies as serious civilization and can offer literature with universal themes. Never mind that this "region" has vast plains, towering mountains, abysmal gorges and flashing rivers to inspire the rebirth of the continental soul. Never mind that the West has the power to expose the tragedy of egocentric materialism, rationalism, and individualism. Never mind that a great Western poet, Robinson Jeffers, expresses a redemptive vision when he writes in *Credo*, "The beauty of things was born before eyes and sufficient to itself; the heart-breaking beauty/Will remain when there is no heart to break for it." Someone back East, who in all other respects might be considered intelligent, will still call the West merely "a state of mind" and see himself far from Zane Grey. Westerners write "Westerns," don't they?

Let us consider the skinniness and aridity of Phaedra Greenwood's home beside the river. Would Henry James have written spellbinding chapters about black widow spiders, tree-felling beavers, and Corn Mother dances? Would it have even occurred to him to ponder the significance of a petroglyph? Would he have dared to swing out over the river on a rope tied to a swingtree, to repair an adobe church, caressing the mud as if it were a woman's body, to live for a spell with filthy hippies in a commune, to chop wood in a blizzard, to hunt elk with a bow, to swim across the icy Rio Grande, to dance naked in celebration of the vernal equinox, or to shove his arm up an ewe's vagina in order to prevent the aborting of her lambs? Even if he had managed to go West and seat himself for a century in a freezing outhouse beside the Rio Hondo, would he have noticed the very real and vital presence of literature?

But look! In the valley D.H. Lawrence is galloping on horseback across a snow-packed road to Taos Pueblo. Cleofas Martínez de Jaramillo, born in Arroyo Hondo in 1878, suffers from no lack of subject matter when she writes *Romance of a Little Village Girl*. Just up the road in Arroyo Hondo lived Frank Waters, one of the greatest American writers of the twentieth century, seven times nominated for the Nobel Prize in Literature. Would Henry James have come to understand that such writers in one little postage stamp of Northern New Mexico were, and are, somewhat more substantial than a state of mind? Would solitude play its music for James' ears, as it does for Greenwood's?

The compulsion to write leads writers, of course, to all sorts of weird places, including England. Writing takes time, writing makes demands on writers and their loved ones, but an author's empty purse is always filled with the intangible wealth of sacrifice and compassion.

Readers of *Beside the Rio Hondo* will realize that Phaedra Greenwood has not swerved from her destiny, has not flinched from its demands, has not begged or borrowed or whimpered, has never strayed from the reign of wonder. Her memoir is a portrait of the artist as a young archetype. Her imagination is inevitably in revolt against the hostile forces that would destroy, through shabbiness and inhumanity, what she loves. So she is faithful to the wounds of life and cannot be discouraged from her task just because she is vulnerable before social, economic and religious, "get-a-real-job" authorities of the tribe. She breaks away from the tribe's daylight world, submerges herself in the sea of images, makes a pilgrimage to the shrines where the truth of her experience lies, and finally, after years of sprightly dancing in a metaphorical wilderness, surfaces with a story that teaches the lesson of life renewed. The archetype is this journey, this night of the soul. The shrines are Time and Place. And the message is: we are never, any of us, really alone.

—Alexander Blackburn

Preface

*I*n our family writing was as ordinary as reading, eating breakfast or taking a bath. Dad struggled for years to write a best seller, pounding out his ire on an old Underwood typewriter. He took odd jobs to support the family, drove a taxi, worked for small-town newspapers and brought home bars of Linotype and newsprint for us to play with. Mother wrote poetry—verse, Dad called it—though it didn't always rhyme.

Every night before we went to bed, Mother read to us—nursery rhymes and fables, then fairy tales, and eventually Anna Sewell's entire book, *Black Beauty*. Then Dad took over and entertained us with junior books, biographies of famous Americans from McGraw-Hill where he worked as a proofreader. On cold autumn nights he provoked nervous giggles from us as he read the morbid tales of Edgar Allen Poe.

Once a week my parents hosted a writer's group in the living room where the walls were lined with books set on Dad's homemade shelves. I got the message early—books are sacred and writers are pilgrims on the long, literary journey, making daily sacrifices on the altar of the word.

My father never published. When he died, at the back of his storage shed, I found bundles of manuscripts three feet high and two feet deep, tied with string. For over two decades he had been writing and rewriting his autobiography, trying to express some essential truth about childhood events that had shaped his life.

I carted home as many bundles of paper as I could stuff in the trunk of my car. It took months to wade through this dark confessional memoir, written in his Hemingway style. Bats, snakes and spiders fell out as I turned the pages. When I couldn't take any more, I dumped most of it in the recycling bin.

Unlike my father, I didn't decide to become a writer—I just wrote. Writing was a way of expressing my feelings and keeping depression at bay, but I seldom made it the center of my life. I opened my arms to husbands and lovers, to children and animals, jobs, travel and outdoor adventures from camping in Alaska to scuba diving in the Caribbean.

In the 1970s and 80s I was a blur as I dashed around trying to save the Earth so that my children and grandchildren might enjoy the beauty of it as much as I did. In those days my best literary efforts went into composing letters to the forest service, congress and newspaper editors protesting nuclear power and nuclear waste, budworm spraying and the pollution of the Rio Hondo. But at night before I rolled into sleep, I grabbed fifteen minutes to jot a few notes in my journal.

Today my stack of journals is eight feet high. From these scribblings I draw fresh details for novels, essays and memoirs, shaping the material to tell the story of my life, which is not just my own story, but also that of my family and community.

In my "getting-on" years I was dismayed to discover my mouse-eaten manuscripts piling up in the trunk, at the back of the shed, under the bed, in every spare closet and drawer. My worst nightmare was coming true: I would die unpublished and unread like my father, my life's work dumped in the hole with me.

So it's deeply satisfying to see—fourteen years after I wrote it—that a segment of my private journal is about to waltz out into the world as my first published book. How strange to realize that I was writing it all along without knowing it.

Beside the Rio Hondo is a work of creative non-fiction that follows the seasons for one pivotal year of my life. In 1992, at the age of 49, I separated from my husband and made a beeline for our family home in Arroyo Hondo, a quiet valley in the mountains of Northern New Mexico. Embracing the emptiness of my nest, I returned to an unfinished task that I had shunned at the age of eighteen: to establish an independent identity. For the first month, alone on the land, deep listening became my daily meditation. Grounded in the solitude of our old adobe on the edge of the national forest, I finally slowed down long enough to experience an epiphany.

The story expands in concentric circles to include the flora and fauna of the high mountain desert, the geology and changing weather patterns, my interaction with the neighbors and notes on the daily struggle to survive. I've added a dash of local history that streaks across the centuries from ancient petroglyphs and pit houses to the wild hippie days during the 1970s when three communes in the area wrestled with rural life.

More than a personal memoir, this book is about the fierce spirit of place, the politics of the tri-cultural community of Hispanos, Indians and Anglos, the give and take that allows us to work and play together, and what it means to belong to the land.

People are hungry for tales that give ordinary life height and breadth and meaning. Creative non-fiction is the lens that focuses the narrative by eliminating extraneous detail, rearranging time sequences to build to a climax and supplying crucial resolution. Yes, it all really happened; more important, the story is true to itself. To paraphrase Iris Keltz in *Scrapbook of a Taos Hippie*, for those of you who experienced it some other way, your version is true, too.

The Hondo Valley

Acknowledgements

*M*any heartfelt thanks to all the readers and writers, friends and family, who have encouraged me to see this manuscript to fruition, especially Alex and Ines Blackburn, Morgan Farley, Terry Lukas, Iris Keltz, John Nichols, Natalie Goldberg, Linda Sonna, Jonna-Lynn Mandelbaum, Jerry Padilla, my sister Carolyn Shortt, and my brother Tom Gore. I also deeply appreciate the time, effort and exceptional talents of the artists Glenda Gloss, Jim Pedersen and Jan Gustafson, who contributed their original work to illustrate this book. For more information on Pendersen, see www. pedersenart.com. My deepest thanks goes to my writing teacher, Laurel Goldman, who for five years saw me through the creative highs and lows and showed me how to spin straw into gold. Also *muchas gracias* to Harvey Mudd whose generosity and friendship helped the Levys establish a family home. And finally, gratitude and love to Jim Levy for believing in my writing and for his patience in proofing and editing this manuscript—over and over again.

Coming Home

I hate moving. When I was a child my family moved about once a year, towing the U-Haul behind the old '39 Pontiac as we wandered from town to town and state to state. Moving is supposed to improve your situation, but the more we moved, the more we lost and left behind. After awhile it felt like running away. I was always "the new girl" with the strange accent and ill-fitting clothes from the local thrift store. Just when I had made a friend, we started packing again. I cringed at the sight of cardboard boxes, dust balls at the back of the closet, empty hangers on the floor. When we took the pictures down, the ghostly rectangles on the walls gave me a queasy feeling. Most of all, I hated saying good-bye. Again. And again. And again.

In my twenties I wanted to get married, buy a few acres of land and settle down somewhere. Forever. I searched the whole country for a place to call home and finally found it in Taos, New Mexico. I enjoyed the fluid sound of Spanish that rippled past me in the stores, and admired the elemental life of the Indians at Taos Pueblo. I liked the adobe architecture that blended with the earth, and the massive mountain peaks towering over the town. Taos was as close as I could get to leaving the country without actually leaving the country.

It was 1969 and I was writing for an alternative paper called *The Fountain of Light* when I met Aaron, who became the editor. He published our stories and essays side by side. We both had boxes full of unpublished novels, short stories and poems, and craved a certain amount of solitude to work. As we got to know each other better, we plunged into intense discussions about literature and life. He introduced me to the genius of D.H. Lawrence and Marcel Proust, and the angst of Malcolm Lowry and Friedrich Nietzsche.

At one point we laughingly agreed we'd rather give up sex than writing. But our lovemaking was so compelling that we decided to make a life together. For the first ten years we stayed put in our little adobe beside the Rio Hondo. The quiet, sunstruck village of Arroyo Hondo, ten miles north of Taos, just suited me. Aaron was working nights as a projectionist in town, which gave him daytime to write and play with the children and me. These were the brightest years of our life together, when Brian and Rachel were small.

But after his mother died, Aaron grew restless and felt the need to prove himself in the world. His mother had been a library volunteer; Aaron volunteered at the library in Taos and eventually became the director. It was a demanding job that included fundraising and lobbying in the legislature. He drove into town almost every day, so it didn't surprise me when he wanted to move to Taos. True, the schools in town would be better for the children, but a sense of disbelief overwhelmed me as I rolled up the rug in the living room and packed the dishes. I would have stayed in Hondo forever.

We lived in Taos for three years, which was a good experience for all of us, but when it was time for Rachel and Brian to go into junior high and high school, we agreed we'd move somewhere else. The next stop was Chapel Hill, North Carolina, where we established residency and saw Brian through high school and into college. Then on to Boulder, Colorado, where we did the same for Rachel.

By then Aaron and I no longer saw eye-to-eye on what we

wanted out of life, and months of expensive marriage counseling didn't help. One thing, in particular, bothered me. Aaron had owned the Hondo property before we were married; my name wasn't on the title. I finally worked up the courage to ask him why. He reminded me that his friend Harvey had sold him the house on the condition that it remain in Aaron's name.

My face went hot; my stomach churned. How could I flourish in a relationship where my husband didn't trust me? The ownership of the Hondo house became symbolic of the many ways I felt disenfranchised in the marriage, left out of decisions large and small that were important to our relationship.

Aaron said that if I wanted equality, I should give up my writing and get a full time job.

I argued that both of us could have worked part time and kept writing if he had been willing to live more economically, meaning if we had stayed in Hondo. I should give up writing so we could live this middle-class life?

Writing ran like a deep river in my family. My grandfather had been a renowned overseas correspondent and columnist for *The Detroit News*. Dad was a frustrated, unpublished novelist, a taxi driver, a boat builder, a Linotype operator and reporter for small town newspapers. At the top of his career he earned a decent living as a proofreader for McGraw-Hill Publishing Company in New York. At the bottom, in his fifties, he slaved as a bus boy working split shifts at a posh restaurant in Hawaii.

My mother took clerical jobs, burned the dinner, wrote poetry. My sister turned out short stories; in later life my brother wrote songs and novellas. From the time I was old enough to clutch a pencil in my fist and scrawl a few letters, I wrote rhymed poems, then short stories. In my twenties my short stories grew into novellas, then full-blown novels.

For years I juggled writing with part-time jobs and family responsibilities. I felt sure that if I had time to focus on my art without any distractions, I could produce something worth reading, but my compulsion to write created too much tension in the family.

When the heat of our quarrels finally drove me out the door, I didn't have the heart to start over in Boulder. Too much traffic. Red brick. Jagged foothills clawing the sky. In the ten years we had been gone I had never stopped dreaming of adobe bricks, dried mud flecked with bits of yellow straw, the walls of our old adobe.

"You can't go back to Hondo," a friend told me. "That's not starting a new life."

"I don't want a new life," I said. "I want to go home."

I needed the soft curves of the Sangre de Cristos to soothe my eyes, the silver thread of the Rio Hondo to mend my days. For me home was a worn path down to the river, bits of green milkglass and pot sherds under my boots; the dailiness of watering the garden, feeding the animals, the fire; practicing Tai Chi beneath the blazing eye of the morning sun. Home was a habit of loving that didn't fade, a tapestry of relationships, events and memories.

I wanted to keep the property not just for me, but for the children—a place where they could take a break from the world, a house where they could bring their children, if they had any, a space for family reunions. I had to find some way to change Aaron's mind, buy him out, or work out a deal with the neighbors. If I couldn't take my last stand in Hondo where my boots had worn a path down to the river, where could I stand?

Aaron thought I was nuts. "You'll have to deal with all that macho stuff by yourself. Not to mention the repairs, the ditch cleaning and the irrigation. And how will you make a living? Taos is the poorest county in the state, and New Mexico has one of the highest unemployment rates in the country."

I shrugged. "They're not unemployed—they're busy. I have the bucket, the shovel and the ax. What more do I need?" I also had dried grains, sixteen quarts of canned apples and cherries, and a three-month-supply of flour, sugar, powdered eggs and milk. I longed for one last summer on the land.

22 ——

We had rented out the house while we were away, so Aaron asked me to pay him two hundred and fifty dollars a month, half the amount we had received from our tenants. Though he had a high-paying job working for the Boulder Housing Authority, I didn't ask for half of our bank account because he was helping the kids through college. I couldn't give them anything but moral support. All I had was my car and a thousand dollars I had saved from a part-time job as administrator at the Unitarian Universalist Church. And my first credit card in my own name.

When I saw that our marriage was not going to survive, I had gone to J.C. Penney's and bought a down comforter on credit. At least I'd have that to keep me warm. I made my monthly payments on time and intended to use this as a reference to apply for a credit card. Six months later, like a miracle, a VISA offer arrived in the mail. I was ready to roll.

Aaron said that if our finances didn't improve, we'd have to sell the house in a year and split the proceeds.

Sell. The word shriveled my heart with fear. He could do it, too, without my consent. The property had once consisted of an eighty-acre strip that ran back up over the top of the mesa to the Forest Service line. The year before we moved to Taos, Aaron had sold the top part; now all we had left were twenty acres of rocky hillside, the house and narrow shelf it sat on, and four acres of irrigated land below.

The day after Rachel graduated from high school, I climbed in my old Toyota and headed south for New Mexico. Brian, home from college for the summer, followed me in the U-Haul with the family dog and two cats. Twenty years of marriage down the drain; I cried all the way out of town.

But my heart began to lift as we labored over La Veta Pass and swooped down into the San Luis Valley, a curving road through a verdant mountain valley. The willows surged in orange and crimson flames along the winding stream. I opened the window and sucked the cool air into my lungs.

At the windswept town of Fort Garland we turned south on Highway 159. This straight stretch of empty road divides potato fields from pale yellow fields of barley that span the distance from the road to the slopes of the Sangre de Cristos, Blood of Christ mountains, the tail end of the Rockies. These mountains are younger and more gently rounded than the sharp, dramatic spine of the fourteeners in Colorado. The uplift of the Sangre de Cristos is about sixty million years old, the same age as Mount Everest.

On the southern horizon, in shifting sunlight, I spied ghostly white peaks, my familiar mountains. The landscape grew more vivid as we approached Taos. Waves of feeling churned through me; this was not a quick three-day visit crammed with friends to call and cleaning and repairs on the house, but a full return home.

Ten miles south of Questa we zoomed down a hill into Arroyo Hondo, a village steeped in tradition, with a mule-like resistance to change. In 1813 forty-four Hispano families requested an edict to grant them land along the Rio Hondo to establish a village and raise their crops and livestock. In 1815, seeing that "it will damage not even the Indians, on account of it being outside of their league," the *Alcalde* (Mayor) of Taos gave possession and grant of approximately 20,629 acres in the name of the King of Spain. (According to SouthwestBooks.org, 30,674 acres were claimed, but only 20,629 confirmed.) The remaining *ejido realengos* or common lands would be used by the village to graze livestock, gather herbs and firewood.

———— ———— ————

We turned at Herb's Lounge and cruised past the small houses strung along the road overlooking the green wedge of river valley. I was aware of the history of many of these families, cycles of drama being played out from generation to generation. I laughed to see the Pachecos' old buckskin still hanging his head over the fence, the Romeros' flock of sheep hiding from the sun in the shadow of a stack of hay bales. Leroy Márquez was out hoeing rows to plant pumpkins in his garden plot and Roy Barela was driving his tractor up and down the field, making his first cut of alfalfa. The damp smell of fresh grass tickled my nose.

Where the road narrowed we crept past *Nuestra Señora de los Dolores*, Our Lady of Sorrows, the first structure to be built by the community about 180 years ago. Solid and beautiful, this traditional adobe church had often been photographed and painted. I had been inside three or four times; the interior was solid and authentic, too. The carved and painted saints of Our Lady of Sorrows represented one of the most important collections of Hispano folk art from any single village in the area. In the evening sunlight the robed figure of the Madonna cast her graceful silhouette on the stained glass window. The surrounding wall was being restored and the north wall of the church still needed mudding. Once I had settled in I could help plaster—if they'd let me.

We turned up the hill into our driveway and home. Brian and I climbed out, hugged each other and stood for a moment enjoying the beauty that unfolded before us, our land that had once been part of the *ejido*, an unfenced triangle of green bounded on the south by the Rio Hondo. The silver river sparkled through the cottonwood trees and dropped in noisy rills as it rushed over smooth stones on its way to meet the Rio Grande. Across the stream, white Arabians grazed in the pasture, swishing their tails. Through the trees I could see a large house with redwood siding, Dr. David and Ellen Cohn, my only visible neighbors. Our children had grown up together; for years Rachel and their youngest daughter Yona were best friends.

Our house sat on a shelf overlooking the river with a steep, boulder-strewn hillside behind it—very Feng Shui. Nestled into its setting, the salmon-pink of the stucco walls stood in soft contrast to the olive-gray sage.

I let the dog out of the truck and carried the cats into the house; Brian helped me unload the U-haul. He was twenty-one, six feet tall, and muscular from jogging and Karate; he could have carried in the few pieces of furniture by himself.

We ate fruit and sandwiches and slept on the floor in our

sleeping bags. In the morning we returned the U-Haul and I drove him to Taos to catch the bus back to Boulder. He planned to spend the summer living with his dad, working as an usher at one of the theaters. In the fall he'd head back to college in North Carolina.

With a waft of diesel and the sound of gravel crunching, Brian's bus pulled in. I kissed his cheek and laughed with surprise at the stubble of his beard. He patted me. "Mom, are you going to be okay here?"

The streets were wet with rain; the sage smelled pungent, familiar. "Please, please, Brer Fox, don't throw me in that briar patch," I laughed.

His tawny eyes were warm with affection. "Keep in touch. You know where I am."

I had his address, but that's not what he meant.

"Where are you, Brian?"

"In the place where all of us are alone."

Alone. The word reverberates through me as I drive home. I stop only to pick up a copy of *The Taos News*. I don't want to see any of my old friends and have to explain why Aaron and I split.

I pull up in the driveway and sit looking at the empty house, dismayed by a sense of alienation. The old *casa* is wrapped in silence, brooding. On previous visits home, between renters, Rachel said, "I've noticed it, too. It's okay once you're inside."

But it's hard to step back into the setting when the house itself refuses to welcome me. I scan the yard as I walk up the path. Nothing has been disturbed since we left this morning, but I am aware of an intricate web of events—feathers on the lawn—life and death dramas I will never know. But the house knows.

Perhaps the old *casa* remembers the family that lived here in the 1920s and 30s. According to Isabel Rendón of middle Arroyo Hondo, this was a three-room house, probably built by José del Carmen Martínez. His daughter, Odila Martínez, was Isabel's first cousin. "I used to go up there all the time," Isabel said.

Odila's mother was Escolastica. It's an unusual name for a woman. *Escolastico* means scholar. Did she like to read?

As Isabel tells the story, Jose and Escolastica first lived with their new baby in middle Hondo, perhaps at Isabel's parent's house, or nearby. It was around 1911 and Escolastica was about twenty. Was she beautiful with long black hair? "We have no pictures of her," Isabel said, but she remembers a big wedding in Arroyo Hondo.

One day Escolastica was baking bread behind the house in an *horno*, an outdoor oven made of adobe mud. When the oven reached the right temperature, she raked out the coals, swept it and put in the loaves.

She must have been high-spirited because she was dancing around the pile of coals, humming to herself, twitching her skirts. A spark flew out and caught her petticoats on fire. Was she alone with the baby? Did she run for the ditch? No use—it was shut down, and hauling water from the well would have taken too long. She went up in a blaze like a human torch.

Isabel's father, Carlos Trujillo, was on his way to town. When he reached the top of the hill he saw the fire. His niece was standing in the yard holding out both arms like a cross, probably signaling for help. For a moment she seemed to lift from the earth.

Carlos turned the wagon around and raced back to the house. He threw a blanket around her and smothered the flames, but she was charred to the skin. It was difficult to separate her from her corset and high-laced boots, Isabel said. "She couldn't stand to have even the sheets touching her." Escolastica died three days later leaving José with the baby. Was he heartbroken? Did he blame himself, thinking he could have saved her if only. . . . If only. . . .

He remarried, of course, and moved to our house with his second wife, Celestina. She helped him to raise Odila, but she was ill, perhaps with leukemia, and she never had any children of her own. They grew corn in the field below the house. They kept horses and cows and butchered their own meat. I can still see the remnants of their barn—stone walls built into the hillside.

At that time their *casa* was the only one on the north side of the river. Someone told me they crossed on a fallen log. It must have been a hard life with no well and an outhouse. The dust, the mud, the stony ground. After awhile they gave it up and moved to Pueblo, Colorado, where José took a job in a steel mill. Odila married a man from Costilla and moved to Avondale, Colorado.

Escolastica. Her story haunts me.

The Hondo House

*A*s I step into the kitchen and yank the cord that turns on the overhead light, I become the dance that keeps this place alive. I know this house from the inside out and I know how to fix it. A good thing, too, because it needs a lot of work. My morning high peters out as I walk around making notes on the materials I'll need for repairs. The silver poplars Aaron and I planted outside the back door have grown higher than the roof, but along the path I find the stones unchanged. I caress their smooth shapes, feel the stored warmth of the sun, but I can't hear their voices anymore. They used to whisper, "Stay. Be still." I will have to learn how to listen again.

Our series of tenants have been hard on the place. One couple with children loved it and wanted to buy it, but others left their garbage in the sheds and bald tires lying in the sun-baked yard. The "lawn" has gone to weeds; the flowerbeds are overgrown. I'm glad we had the house stuccoed. No way we could have kept up the mudding while we were gone. That crack around the chimney needs tar so the rain won't seep through and wash away the adobe underneath. The roof of the shed is rotten and leaks, and the outhouse is sinking backward into its own hole.

Inside, the house looks as if it hasn't been thoroughly cleaned since we moved out. The rafters we call *vigas* are thick with dust; windows are broken, doors won't lock. My rocking chair is trashed. I swallow hard as I toss its broken legs into the wood pile, remembering the icy winter nights I nursed my babes in this chair, half asleep, rocking, rocking.

I walk down to the orchard. Last spring the ditch association took out our leaky headgate to the Atalaya Ditch, so there's no way to divert water into my lateral ditches to irrigate. We have only five apple and two apricot trees left. I tell them they're on their own.

At night I lie in the back bedroom of the L-wing gazing up at the chip marks of Aaron's adz where he stripped the bark from the *vigas*. The protective strength and energy he put into building this part of the house makes me feel secure. I wish I could pick up the L-wing like a genie and set it in a clearing on the rocky hillside where I'd have a perfect view of the mountains. Then Aaron could sell the rest of the house and bottom acres; I'd be content up there.

In the morning the sun glows across bright fields wet with rain; I smell adobe and sage. I squat in the grass and pee, marking my territory. Our big German Shepherd, Ocho, and the two cats, Snuggles and Samantha, hover around the house waiting to see what I'll do next. I stand in the driveway, barefoot, the wind blowing through my thin nightgown, turning slowly in a circle of mountains. "Yes! This is for me." To the east nine miles away rises Wheeler Peak, 13,161 feet, the highest point in New Mexico. The dramatic crags around the peak were sculpted by glaciers that melted about twelve thousand years ago. To the southwest are the Jemez Mountains, their upper slopes still bright with snow. To the west I can see the Brazos uplift, a low line of mountains that circles to the north. My spirit expands to fill the space.

I start cleaning the kitchen. When I dust the *vigas* above the stove I am chagrined to see a thin crust of pea soup still clinging to the ceiling. I scrape it again as if I can purge it from the record. Rachel was four years old, skipping past the stove, when the pressure cooker blew. Fragments of metal and boiling soup flew all over the kitchen. The handle of the lid stuck in the ceiling. She screamed and covered her face. I flew to her, heart pounding, afraid to look. Had I blinded her? Or scalded her for life?

Under the cool water of the bathroom sink she calmed down, but my hands were shaking. Thick waves of honey-colored hair had saved her face; only a few drops had splattered her cheek. I never used a pressure cooker again.

I've been home for two weeks. It was completely overcast when I woke up this morning, gloomy outside and in. I feel sad when I look at the trampoline sitting out there. Brian and Rachel and their friends aren't going to come and jump on it. Or are they? Is part of me hoping to bring the family back together by restoring the nest? Don't think it. Stay present.

But it's hard when I feel anxious about money. If Aaron decides to sell the house next year, I'll have to move again. Right now my body is so sore I can't bear the thought. I'm cut, scratched and bruised from scrubbing, hammering and vacuuming. When I leaned on the outside table, the legs dropped off; the benches fell apart when I picked them up. Last night during a storm the top pane of my bedroom window blew onto the floor with a crash. It had been held in—who knows for how long?—with duct tape. I fixed locks and hinges, replaced broken windows and frames.

I've abandoned the master bedroom—too many memories—and made my nest in the L-wing at the back of the house. My desk stands under the window looking out at the longbow of pale mountains on the western horizon, mussel shell blue. I cover my bed with a spread of magenta and indigo; by coincidence the curtains match. The room feels peaceful. I caress the bare white wall, the curve and swell of plaster over adobe bricks, the contours I made with my bare hands when I plastered these walls eighteen years ago.

The day before we moved to Taos Aaron said, "Our renters aren't going to appreciate that messy molding in the hall. Better pull it off and replace it." Instead, I turned its face to the wall but didn't nail it down. Today I turned it over and inspected it under the lamp. Almost forty lines are drawn across it in pencil or pen, recording the date and height of each person—friends and neighbors, adults and growing children—beginning with a line at the bottom when Brian was only twenty-five inches high. Suddenly the hall is crowded with ghosts, rulers resting on their heads, fidgeting and blushing, trying to look tall. And I am filled with a rush of longing to invite all of them back to be measured again.

By late afternoon I'm sticky and exhausted. I take a walk down the driveway. A storm sweeps in from the west, thunder over the mountains; a few drops make miniature craters in the soft dust. It smells good. This is how clouds are supposed to look—puffy and rolling, with sweeping veils of rain.

It must be Sunday. I heard the church bell ring at 8:30 and felt lonely, but not lonely enough to call anyone. I didn't put on my watch all day and I've lost track of the date. I'm walking around barefoot in a T-shirt and underpants, vacuuming and nailing. How many times have I spruced up this house for a new tenant? This time, as I complete each room, waxed, polished and repaired, I raise my hands and pronounce it, "Mine!"

Waking up alone in this house, I can't help thinking, Yes, I can make it beautiful again, but what for? All these empty rooms filled with sunlight and the sound of the river. I do want the beauty and spirit of the land, but do I want the ongoing struggle to keep this house from sinking into the ground? I'll probably run out of money by Christmas. I have to find a job, create community. How do I make a new life in this isolated place? Big question. I'd better figure it out fast.

The Song of the Stones

I was out in the studio repainting the floor when I heard shrill voices down by the Rio Hondo. I stood in the door watching. Three boys from the village were splashing in a pool beneath a huge boulder lodged into the south bank of the stream. Their voices struck a keen note: "Catch him! Catch him!"

Should I go down? None of my business. Or was it? I started down the hill, hands in my pockets. What should I say? The oldest boy, about twelve, was on his knees ducking his bare shoulders beneath the icy water as he groped under the rock. The younger boys, about eight or nine, stood ankle-deep in the stream, egging him on. I nodded hello and stood watching. It's no easy feat catching a trout with your bare hands, but the oldest boy had already tossed a couple of six or seven inch browns on the bank. I interrupted them long enough to introduce myself and ask their names.

"Luis," the oldest one said.

"Pancho."

"Felipe."

"Are you from the village?"

They looked blank. I motioned toward the church with my thumb and they nodded.

"Please throw the fish back if they're too small. Don't waste them." As an afterthought I said, "If you have any big ones left over, I'll buy them from you. I live in that house up on the hill."

After I left they grew quiet, moved upstream. An hour later they came marching up the hill and stood in line at my door, Luis first, the smallest boy last, savage hunters turned merchants, for better or worse. Luis was shivering. The younger ones were sunny and innocent, soft-cheeked with eyes like birds, looking up at me expectantly. Luis opened his pack and showed me three little fish.

"How much?" I said.

"Five."

Felipe's eyes lit up, "Ten!"

I shook my head. "They're pretty small. I'll give you a dollar apiece."

They eyed each other, mouths twisting, then took it, as I knew they would. They peeked in the window while I went to get my purse. I gave the money to Luis. He handed the younger boys a dollar each and asked what days I was home. "Every day," I said.

I asked if they had blessed the fish or thanked them for their lives. They looked at me, big-eyed, "No."

After they left, I sat down at the round blue table under the *portal* (porch) to write about them in my journal. Lately I have been hearing myself say, "If I don't write about it, it doesn't mean anything." I ponder that. Not that raw life in its essence is meaningless, but that consciousness through writing, through art, is really the goal here. My intuitive sense says to get my life in balance, in order. Let go of the old to make room for the new, whatever form that may take.

I need to slow down, take time to look at things, appreciate what's around me. Here I am in this beautiful setting, working until I fall down at night, getting up the next day, doing it again. I'm so busy I don't have time for my feelings; loneliness is bound to be one of them. Learning how to be alone is what I'm moving toward, to be with my own silence, to hear my own voices.

In the late afternoon I whistle to Ocho and climb a rough track that cuts across the rocky hillside behind the house, a gradual ascent as it parallels the river. It's a south-facing slope, sunny and free of snow most of the winter. This is an old wagon road once used by the locals to get to the top of the mesa to cut firewood. Even when the road was passable, it must have been a bumpy ride and dangerous coming down with a load of piñon.

In the bareness of these hills dotted with piñon and juniper, I have begun to notice every nuance of humankind's intermingling with the land from an occasional basalt arrowhead to the faded stumps of trees that were hewn with an ax a hundred years ago.

The vegetation—what there is of it—is Upper Sonoran. Dry branches of sage have been twisted like driftwood by the west wind. Botanists have counted their rings and discovered some are nearly seven hundred years old. In my hand I turn the woody skeleton of the walkingstick cholla, once used for canes, a hollow cylinder with a diamond mesh.

A dash of purple vetch catches my eye. The mesa is coming into bloom. I thrill to the delicate spikes of Indian paintbrush aflame in the slanting rays of the sun. Wisps of pale yellow grama grass offset the heaviness of brown, basalt boulders. The prickly pear spread their waxy yellow blossoms wide for the bees.

In a cleft at the base of a boulder where it catches the runoff, a Spanish bayonet radiates sharp spikes. Around here we call them yucca. This one may thrust up a tall stalk massed with pale yellow flowers. The Indians stripped fibers from the spikes to weave a coarse fabric; the roots were used for shampoo.

I cut through the sandy arroyo and climb uphill. Staring at the ground I try to read the history of the stones, to understand what happened here. In the heart of the Jemez Mountains west of the Rio Grande about a hundred miles away, an immense volcano, perhaps over twenty thousand feet high, once dominated the landscape.

When it exploded a million years ago the blast left an empty crater, a caldera twelve miles across, and littered the countryside with volcanic debris. Other smaller volcanoes contributed, as well. This area has a two billion year history of repeated uplift and erosion, a profusion of volcanoes and lava flows, and fault scarps where the mountains join the plateau. The last uplift began seventy million years ago and continues today.

These basalt boulders on the hillside are pocked volcanic rock, their sides mottled with pale green and splashes of bright orange lichen. Sometimes I sprawl across them, hug them, absorb their warmth. They are constant lovers, here for me in all seasons. These bones of the earth feel solid and reassuring against my hands.

Speak to me! Stone truth. Tell me if this is where I belong.

They sing of volcanic fire, the original explosion, the final return.

"Climb up here," says the rocky point. I pull myself up the last few feet. My forehead is damp. A light wind cools my cheeks.

Lookout Point

I stand looking at the mountains in the far distance, and for a few moments I feel frightened—I'm so cut off. On the edge of nowhere, like planet Earth on the edge of the Milky Way. I think about "order" and then "chaos," Aaron's word for the unpredictable element of this place, the sudden violence, the number of unsolved murders of women in Taos.

From this natural lookout point I can see east to the deep cleft in the mountain where the Rio Hondo emerges to wind through the tablelands of Valdez. Cloud shadows drift across the mountainside. The land is wild and beautiful, with weathered slopes spreading out in alluvial fans.

To the west lie orderly patches of irrigated fields bound by dark rows of trees that line the *acequias*, the irrigation ditches. Dirt roads converge in the heart of the village. From a cluster of lime-green poplars, rises the shining roof and bell tower of Our Lady of Sorrows and a block or so to the west, the red roof of the Hondo-Seco fire station.

My eye glides across the hazy mesa and leaps the dark chasm of the Rio Grande Gorge to the low swell of the volcanic range that reels in the horizon thirty miles away. Out there is Tres Orejas, a rag-tag community of artists, eccentrics and old hippies living off the grid on faith, solar power and anarchy, on Buddhism and rainwater.

Annual rainfall here is about twelve inches, but no one knows anymore when "the monsoons" will come. Back in the seventies when we still had predictable rainfall patterns, winter snow gave way to a dry, dusty spring. Around the Fourth of July, when most of the snow had melted off the peaks, the afternoon rains commenced.

Weather here is so localized that it might be raining in Taos, San Cristobal and all around, while not a drop is falling in Hondo. On the other hand, it might rain in Hondo and nowhere else.

Aaron and I used to watch the afternoon clouds sail in from a hundred miles away. Rain cooled the Sandías and flushed the arroyos in Albuquerque by two-thirty. Around three o'clock sudden showers scattered the tourists on the plaza in Santa Fe. An hour later the storm swept toward Taos trailing gray veils we call virga and the Indians call "walking rain."

I ran to get the laundry off the line as the first big drops made miniature craters in the soft dust of our driveway. A blaze of lightning, a boom of thunder, and the torrents let loose. A ten-minute deluge refreshed the garden, tamped down the dust and left the air cool and pungent with the scent of ozone and sage.

Then a flood of sunlight pierced through the edge of the cloud, streaking the fields lime green. Wet with rain, the trunk of our giant tree glowed like a Rembrandt painting with ocher and burnt sienna against ink-black shadows. The clouds thinned to reveal the peaks and a double rainbow arched across the valley from hill to hill.

"Come look at this!" Aaron would call me to the door where we stood grinning, arms locked around each other, sniffing the air. These were the moments we lived for. A change of weather, clouds and clearing, brought color and a clarity of light that stopped us in our tracks about twice a week.

From this jutting rock, circled by a ring of mountains, the San Luis Basin looks like an archipelago washed by an ocean of sagebrush and sand. Until late Mesozoic time this part of the Southwest was alternately land and sea, as the shoreline advanced and retreated over a low-relief landscape. During Pennsylvanian time, eighty percent of New Mexico was submerged beneath warm, shallow, equatorial seas much like the flat coastal plain of modern-day North Carolina. In the long, afternoon wind I can still feel the ebb and sway of the ocean.

I suck in a startled breath. To my left, on a vertical rock facing the river, I discover a large double spiral pecked on the stone, an ancient petroglyph. I kneel beside it and trace the lines with my finger. Some archeologists say the spiral is a symbol of emergence, of water and light, the forces of the universe in motion.

Many tribes consider lookout points sacred features of the landscape. The "ancient ones" must have climbed up here, just as I have, to contemplate the vast circle of land and sky and watch for raiding tribes. Where the village baseball diamond is now, the indigenous people cleared fields to plant corn. To water, they channeled run-off from the arroyos; these were the first *acequias*. They hunted rabbits and deer, kept turkeys in pens and still had enough leisure time to peck away the patina on many boulders in this valley. They created clusters of petroglyphs on south-facing rocks, usually overlooking water, perhaps to honor specific sites for a certain event that happened there, or to signify that the site itself is sacred.

The "ancient ones" supposedly migrated here from Chaco Canyon nine hundred years ago during a period of prolonged drought. Their stone structures at Chaco were so elaborate and sophisticated that archeologists found it hard to believe that the same people would build crude pit houses on the ridges. Were these immigrants like the pioneers who built sod houses and rustic cabins on the Western frontier?

Later, as their numbers increased, they moved down into the valley and lived above ground in a small pueblo community across from my house called El Pueblito.

All the sites around here have been thoroughly investigated and there are no more plans to dig, but last fall when a human skull washed out of the hillside into the Hondo-Seco Road, archeologists were called to excavate the grave. The bones, about six hundred years old, were from a fifty-two year old man. At the top of the grave they found, intact, an elaborately painted black and white urn. The elders from Taos Pueblo, who claim the people of El Pueblito as their ancestors, have asked for the bones so they can re-inter them in a special ceremony.

I've heard that every year natives from Taos Pueblo follow the old trails north on horseback to Questa to collect ceremonial red clays. Maybe that's what they were doing that August day I hiked through the canyon into Valdez to the broken walls of Turley's Mill.

In the 1800s, using surplus grains grown in Taos valley, Simeon Turley made a popular brew called "Taos Lightning." He was murdered during the Taos Revolt of 1847, a Hispano and Indian rebellion against the United States. Today all you can see of the old mill are the remnants of sturdy rock walls.

I was contemplating the hefty stones when I was startled by hoofbeats trotting down the dirt road on the south side of the river. I ducked behind a tree. Four Indians wrapped in checked J.C. Penney's blankets rode to the bank of the river and dismounted.

Two of them knelt and drank from the stream with cupped hands; the other two lay flat on their bellies and sipped the cold water with their mouths. I had never seen anyone drink from the Rio Hondo. Time rolled away like a ground fog, thinning, dispersing. I could hear the voices of the "ancient ones" rising from the earth itself, whispering over the rocks and through the twisted cedars. My psyche plunged through a *sipapu* hole into the still center where everything changes and stays the same like the bright pattern of water over stones.

I'm awake in the middle of the night again. I have forgotten the silence so thick my ears reverberate with the coursing of my blood, all night, threaded through with the sound of the river— SSSShhhhh. I have forgotten the darkness, thick as tar, the hum of crickets.

I stand in my open bedroom door looking out into the back yard. Framed by blowing silver poplars, the gaudy spangled stars of the Big Dipper fill the whole sky like Van Gogh's painting, "Cypresses by Moonlight." I listen. For what? Voices in the tunnels underground? I don't know. I feel something coming. Walls thinning. Eyes watching me.

I work until I run out of steam. The day is over. I flop down on my bed. The heat of desire rises through the soft fabric of my jeans. Is that what this restlessness is about? Wanting a man?

My instincts are all saying hold the space, hold the time. It's sacred. It is. There's a special purpose and meaning in being alone. It's a luxury.

For an hour I watch the creamy trapezoid of sunlight move across the wall as the sun sets. The walls reflect lavender and blue from the bed and curtains. The heart-shaped leaves of the philodendron are illuminated like an illustration in a book. Outside my bedroom door sun-burnished grasses wave in the wind. Cricket hum lulls me. I am still.

———— ———— ————

I've never been alone this long. I've started babbling to myself, the animals, the insects, the birds, the clouds. While I was hemming curtains I heard myself saying, "If I were you, my dear—and for all practical purposes, I am . . ." I smiled and let that revolve through me, wondering at the duality, one giving the other advice.

At night, alone in the house, I feel scared. My neighbors are too far away to hear me scream. My night fears are amorphous, groping for something to glom onto. A bug crawls into my hair. My fear says, "Black widow!" I lurch up and turn on the light. A moth. Just as I'm falling asleep, it happens again.

If you're so scared, go out—face it.

I scoop up my quilt and pillow and stumble out to sleep on the trampoline. It's a moonlit night with a few clouds gliding lazily across the stars. The cats spring up, bouncing me awake. Snuggles, my old black cat, was a kitten when I first brought her home to this house. Sam is from Boulder, striped, lithe and feral. At the slightest alarm, she scrambles up the porch pole onto the roof. Ocho sleeps right under me, which should be reassuring, but she keeps growling at something on the hillside. Around four in the morning the coyotes go crazy up there—cries that pierce the air, shrill, hysterical. As the morning star fades into the delicate pink of dawn, I plunge into a deep sleep.

On my afternoon walk I explore the twisting labyrinth of what I call Tecolote (owl) Canyon. The walls of this side canyon are no more than thirty feet high, cinnamon-colored basalt spattered with green lichens, the crevasses decorated with sprigs of lemon cinquefoil.

The sandy floor is littered with boulders and an occasional pinecone from a ponderosa pine. After a heavy storm, the *arroyo* drains the mesa and pours muddy water into the Rio Hondo. I am treading softly on the sand, coming around a bend into the canyon proper when I hear a trilling. An owl takes off right ahead of me—a huge wingspread, four feet across. I know I'll see it again when I come around the next bend, and there it is perched on a rock no more than fifteen feet away. Again, the trilling sound.

"I know I'm an intruder here," I say. "But I'm just passing through." It lets loose a reddish-yellow stream—quite impressive and definitely territorial—and flies off.

I glance up. A young owl with white down wafting from its head is paralyzed on the ledge a few feet above me, its eyes wide with fright. I say, "Hello, don't be afraid." It looks down shyly. "*Tecolote*," I whisper. "*Tecolote.*"

I was sitting at the outside table playing my guitar and singing to Snuggles the chorus of "Mockingbird Hill" when I saw someone stride across the field next door with a dog at her heels. I recognized her by the thrust of her body, head up, chest out, a stride of confidence and physical well-being, a young Amazon with purity of purpose—Gillian. She is the Cohns' oldest daughter, Brian's age, just back from Africa by way of Israel, checking out her Jewish roots. I couldn't resist going down to see her.

I followed her around "helping" her feed the horses as she told me about her trip to Africa, how good it feels to be home. "The city makes your body feel large and your mind feel small," she said.

"But here your body feels small and your mind feels large."

She nodded toward the green pastures and distant mountains. "This is a place I can relate to. I draw my identity from it."

"Yes."

The land gives you room to expand—the stars, the sound of the river, the slow turn of the days, the approach of clouds from a distance. The land itself is what drew me here, for its own purposes, not mine.

Sunday. Even though I don't leave the property, I am aware of a lull in the village. I take the whole day off, sit on the front step for over an hour watching until I become one with the American kestral. I first spotted it with the binoculars in the top of the cottonwood tree. Against the glare of the morning sun, I can see a glowing orange nimbus around its head and the electric-blue outline of its wings. It soars with wings and tail fanned like a snow angel. I follow its shrill, descending cry, discover the dead tree where it lives. An hour later, it flies over and perches on the telephone wire in front of the house where it sits for a long time, watching the world go by. I am excited by the delicate beauty of its feathers, rusty red and smoky blue with black accents. Its breast is cream-colored, dotted with rust spots; its dark wing feathers are precisely outlined with white.

Snuggles and Ocho lie nearby, watching me watching the hawk watching the valley. Animals do a lot of this—they're not hunting all the time. I take my cue from them. Like St. Thomas Aquinas, I want divine leisure, time to contemplate in deliberate slowness, savoring every aspect of color and flavor, smell and taste.

I'm so slowed down I'm seeing everything in vivid detail. It's dream-like. Lucid morning light and the fresh, damp smell of the earth, every nubble of plaster in the wall distinct, the sparrow hawk singing from the top of the chimney. Brilliant magenta cholla blossoms on the hillside caught in a swirl of white cabbage butterflies.

This old shed I pass at least twice day without a second glance is a natural work of art. The pine boards are deeply grooved, rust-red with pale yellow boles in the center. I plunk myself down in the grass to admire the color.

Dark clouds roll in, moisture in the air and the honest smells of sage, cut hay and horse manure. I can feel the huge earth turning into the breath of the wind. Timeless. Forever. Turning. I am not turning it. It is turning through me, with me. It's very odd. It's a place I've never been—always been. The edge and the center simultaneously. Calm. There's no place I have to be, nothing I have to do. No one to answer to. I'm completely free. All I want to do is loll around in the grass, feel the wind on my arms, smell the salt on my skin. Watch the clouds pile up on the mountains; admire the brilliant red of the geranium against the blue and white of the window frame; wade into the sandy stream bed and take pictures of the golden ripple patterns that stream off my bare toes; write; talk to the animals; climb up on the roof and caress the curves of the mountains with my eyes.

Am I really here? How long can I get away with it? Today was long. Very long. Minute by minute, hour by hour. Like the animals, I moved around, paused, sat, looked. Looked. Fell asleep. Ate. Moved around. It seems strange to be so free, without pressure, limits, desires, demands. Everywhere I look it's so beautiful I want to cry. If only I could figure out how to stay here for the rest of my life.

Poco a Poco

*T*his morning when I poked my head out the back door I saw a man walking toward me along the driveway with a shovel over his shoulder. Eloy claims he was just walking along the ditch minding his own business when I came out and yelled at him for trespassing on my property.

Yelled? I deny it.

The driveway runs behind the house two yards from my bedroom door, so I had been trying to discourage the traffic, especially cars that drove through the orchard to the river and packed the earth so hard I couldn't maintain my feeder ditches. I didn't want an ugly road through our narrow wedge of orchard; I wanted the grass to grow back softly green the way it was when the trees were first planted.

People had gotten used to coming and going as they pleased; what had begun as a road for ditch equipment was on the way to becoming a public thoroughfare if I didn't do something about it. Except for ditch maintenance, my idea of public access is the path beside the river, not the driveway past my bedroom door.

My strategy is to greet the intruder with a smile, offer my hand and introduce myself, then ask who they are and what they're doing. If they're driving a car or riding a four-wheeler, I say, "You're welcome to come through to the river, but please leave your vehicle by the outhouse and walk."

Eloy was already walking. "Good morning," I said, with a smile.

He planted his shovel and offered me a work-callused hand. "*¿Cómo estás?*"

"*Muy bien,*" I said. "Are you here on ditch business?"

"I'm irrigating today so I had to open up the headgate to let more water through. I'm your neighbor at the other end of the valley. My name is Eloy Mascareñas."

He wore a white T-shirt and jeans, hard-topped boots and a billed cap that said, "Wildlife Guides & Outfitters." He was a few inches taller than I, and solidly built. Through his sunglasses his deep brown eyes glimmered with amusement as if I were a cat standing off a dog. "Are you Aaron Levy's wife?"

"Ex-wife. I'm Phaedra Greenwood."

"I thought this house was sold.

"No. I came back."

"Those beavers have been busy. One of those cottonwoods is chewed half way through. You've got quite a pile of willows on your bank. Want me to take those away for you?"

"How much?"

He shook his head. "I'll do it just to help you out. I think *vecinos* should help each other. I try to be a good neighbor."

He took off his cap and slapped it against his thigh. His hair was thick and black like an Indian's and his cheeks were red. His ears stuck out like two pink seashells. He wiped his face. "It's hot today. Can I have a drink?"

"Sure." I led him around to the front of the house. "Would you rather have a beer or a soda?"

"I'll take a glass of cold water if you have some."

We sat in the shade of the porch. I had just finished painting the outside table sky blue to match the window frames. Eloy chattered for fifteen minutes without a pause. "I was born in this valley," he said.

"Do you have a family?"

"No. I don't approve of kids who get married right out of high school. I went to Colorado Springs for awhile with my girlfriend, but I didn't like it. She wanted me to dress up in a clean shirt every day and go to work in an office, but I said the hell with that." He covered his mouth. "Sorry—the heck with that. So I came home. I run about twenty head of cattle. When I need money, I just sell one."

He eyed my green meadow. "You could have a little flock of sheep down there."

I shook my head. "The neighborhood dogs would kill them."

I gave Eloy a guided tour of the house. "The front part is about eighty years old. The back three rooms Aaron and I built together. I'm trying to preserve this as a traditional adobe."

"It's very beautiful," he said. "Do you have any odd jobs you need done?"

"I need some help putting in a new headgate. I can't pay you much but if I get some apples I'll give you some."

"That would be good. I have some pipe lying around that we could use. I'll cap the end and it won't leak at all. But you'll have to wait until the ditch is shut down. They're going to be doing some work on it next week."

He told me to call Ted Green, a plumber and treasurer for the Atalaya Ditch Association, who agreed to bring me some plastic pipe I could use for a siphon. He even helped me get it going—a feat in itself. We had to plug the ends, fill it from a hole in the middle, then run and unplug both ends simultaneously. It worked for a couple of days, then died of air leaks.

Eloy suggested we clear the basins around the trees. Elated to have some help, I grabbed the rake and followed him down to the orchard. It was useless for me to try to dig in this stony ground. When I jumped on the shovel, I fell over. As I cleared the leaves and debris with a rake, Eloy talked non-stop. His shovel bit into the ground and he drove it deep with his heavy work boot.

"People around here don't like me much. I don't hang out in the bars and drink with them. I've seen what it does to people. I don't want to be like that."

"Good for you."

"I don't really care what people think of me. My brothers are my best friends. We do everything together."

"How many do you have?"

"Four. And one sister. All the rest of them are married and have children."

"Why aren't you?"

He stopped to wipe away a trickle of sweat. "I take care of my parents, take them to the doctor, pay the bills." He described their house, the one by the duck pond with the stately rack of elk antlers over the gate. I had often wondered who lived there. "My grandma was a full-blooded Indian from Picuris Pueblo and my Grandpa on my dad's side was part Indian, too. I think most of us have some Indian blood."

I nodded. I didn't have the nerve to claim my Indian heritage and be labeled a Wannabe. "Me—I'm a wildflower in the cultural garden."

"You should be proud of what you are, no matter what you are. My brothers and I run a guide service. We take people hunting and fishing. I own some land up on the mesa. I'm building my house. I don't have time for a girlfriend."

I smiled. "How old are you?"

"Twenty-five."

I shook out my aching arms and looked down the channel he had just finished. "It would have taken me an hour to do that."

He held up one finger. "*Poco a poco se anda lejos.*"

"What does that mean?"

"Little by little we go far. You have to have patience, *mi amiga.*"

"Tell the trees."

He patted my shoulder. "You worry too much."

Our heads swiveled simultaneously toward a rumbling sound. Down the driveway into the orchard came a man in a pickup. Eloy set down his shovel and walked over to the truck. I listened to a muted exchange in Spanish and caught the tone. I went on raking. In a few minutes Eloy returned. "That's Armando Abeyta, the *mayordomo* in charge of the ditch."

"What did he say?"

"He wanted to know why I was helping you."

"What did you say?"

"Because you need water for your orchard."

———— ———— ————

Eloy decided I should have a garden. He picked out a spot behind the house. The stones flew over his shoulder as he told me about his camping trip alone in the mountains fifty miles west of here. While he was in his tent, a mountain lion paid him a visit. "I could hear it sniffing around out there."

"Did you go out?"

"You have to. It's hot in there."

"Did you see it?"

"No, it was gone, but I know that's what it was. I grew up hunting with my grandpa and my dad," he said. "At first you just walk around with the men. You start with a slingshot, then a bow, then a .22, then a bigger gun. By the time you're twelve years old you really know what you're doing."

Every fall he goes bow hunting to give the deer or elk a better chance. "I don't shoot unless I'm sure I can hit them. I usually get my deer or elk the first day."

"How do you get close enough to shoot?"

"I know how to call in an elk with a bugling sound you raise from deep in your throat. I use every part of the animal," he said. "I don't waste anything. I'm making a chandelier out of elk antlers. I tan the hides. One of my brothers is a taxidermist. He mounts the heads."

In twenty minutes he had turned over a plot about ten by ten feet and left big clumps of dirt for me to take out. Then he brought me a load of manure and helped me fence the garden to keep the deer out.

"What can I give you in return?" I asked. "Sewing?"

"I do that myself. I have a sewing machine."

"Cooking?"

"I'm a good cook," he said. "Someday I'll take you fishing. We'll catch a bunch of big trout and roast them over the fire. There's nothing that tastes better than that. But when those apples are ripe you can give me some."

The Spider

*T*his afternoon I turned over an old wooden trunk and found a black widow spider suspended in one corner. I wound up her web on the end of a pencil. She bolted into the corner, turned belly up and waited for me to decide her fate.

I found a jar, nudged her into it, fastened the lid securely and walked down the driveway to the old stone wall. I watched the spider rappel on her spinner, land on a rock and disappear into a crevice.

Old adobes are semi-permeable barriers to the outdoors—drier than camping but not totally secure. It's easy for a spider to crawl up the outside wall and through the gap under one of the long windows. I've been exporting black widows for years. There's no keeping them out. The question is how to live with them?

As a wary mother of two small children, armed with *A Golden Guide to Spiders*, I studied their ways. Like many poisonous species, there is something distinct about their appearance, like bold caps with exclamation marks. There's a word for it—"aposematic". The mature *Latrodectus mactans* has a round, shining body often described as a "shoe button," something Granny must have worn on her high-topped boots. The black widow's legs are long and graceful, tapering to points. A telltale red hourglass decorates her belly, as if God has marked her for all of nature to recognize and respect.

The book says the female rarely leaves her web. When she does, she crawls awkwardly, unlike hunting spiders that dart around catching insects. Adult males wander around searching for females but don't feed or bite. In my house both sexes get equal treatment.

The female builds messy webs, tangles of triangles that you could mistake for cobwebs except for their silken shine. After she mates with the wandering, fasting male, she eats him and becomes "a widow." Their immature offspring may confuse you because they have white and yellow stripes and spots.

Once the "widow" is set up in the corner of my window or cupboard, behind the toilet or under the sink, she is content to fast, meditate and wait for whatever comes her way. The only time you're in danger is in the fall when the spiders start migrating into the house. Some seasons they are more plentiful than others, but the first or second frost puts an end to their wanderings.

One September morning years ago I sucked in my breath as a black widow the size of a hazelnut crawled out from under the refrigerator and headed for my golden-haired cherub who sat on the kitchen floor playing with his blocks. It's these stumbling collisions that cause them to bite. Three victims I've heard about pulled on their jeans and were bitten in the backside. The others were bitten as they lay asleep in bed. It's not fair. You ought to be safe in your own bed.

A black widow bite itself is not painful and may even go unnoticed, but her poison can kill a small child, or an ill or aging adult. The spider book says the severe abdominal pain may be mistaken for appendicitis. The victim may have aching muscles and pain even in the soles of the feet, but no swelling around the bite. The patient sweats and salivates, then goes dry-mouthed, develops swollen eyelids and "usually recovers after several days of agony."

By coincidence, while I was working on this chapter, my hiking buddy Chandra told me how she had snagged a pair of jeans from the laundry basket, pulled them on and felt something sting her hip. She shook out a spider but didn't know what it was. She called the emergency room.

"Do they have an antidote?" I asked.

"Yes, but there are side effects to that, too, so if you're a healthy adult they prefer that you tough it out," she said. "They told me spider bites are over-rated and I wasn't going to die, but I would probably notice the effects in a couple of hours."

She was so nonchalant about it that she went to a movie. "It hit me while I was sitting there," she said. "I had stomach cramps so bad I had to get up and leave. I could hardly walk."

This was followed by a night of such severe pain that she couldn't sleep. Toward morning a friend found her dazed and helpless and took her to a doctor who prescribed Demerol, a narcotic. She took one, sank under its influence, and didn't come up for a week.

A ton of prevention doesn't always prevent a bite. At first I took the Findhorn approach to black widows—I spared them all, talked to the mother of all spiders and tried to make a deal—don't bite any of mine and I won't crush any of yours. I carried them to the stone wall and told them not to come back, "or any of your offspring."

When that didn't work, I resorted to ritual, circling the house with a candle and chanting. But when two-year-old Rachel found one in the corner of her bedroom window I sprayed all the windowsills with Raid.

By fall the house seemed to be infested with black widows. Where could I go to get away from them? I felt safe in the shower but when I glanced up I saw one dangling from the *viga*. I said to Aaron, only half in jest, "Let's move into a motel until Thanksgiving."

He wasn't scared of them, but I became obsessed with these elegant black arachnids. I wondered if I could touch one without being bitten. I dreamed that a black widow was suspended over my head. I wrote about it in my poetry group. That night, sitting up in bed writing in my journal, I felt something on my hair moving toward my forehead on long, delicate legs.

I slid out of bed, strode to the mirror and tipped my head forward. In the mirror I saw a shining black widow suspended over my third eye. When it landed on the dresser I smashed it with a Kleenex box. So much for the Findhorn approach.

If they're quietly settled in a corner for the winter, I'll ignore them. When I want them to leave in the spring, all it takes is a flashlight and an eviction notice: "If you're still here when I come back tomorrow, I'm going to vacuum you up." When I come back the next day, they're gone.

No one in my house has ever been bitten, though once a visitor woke up, turned on her light and screamed as a black widow paraded across her pillow. I have nothing but empathy for any guest who wants to sleep in my zip-up tent in the middle of the living room. Shake it out and move over—I'm coming in.

The Battle of the Beaver

I went down to look at the apple trees today. The leaves looked dusty, droopy; the branches are thick with bright green nubs that will be apples in the fall if I can get water to the trees. I decided to call Armando, the *mayordomo,* to get permission to shut down the ditch for one day so Eloy could help me install a headgate.

I climbed the embankment behind the house and fought my way through the brush to make sure the ditch was running. A glassy ribbon of water five feet wide flows silent and serene through a shady tunnel of willows. This is the Acequia Atalaya. *Atalaya* means watchtower, a fitting name for a ditch that seems to run slightly uphill until you have a fine view a hundred feet above the valley floor.

The Atalaya is about four miles long from the diversion near Tecolote Canyon to the lower end of Hondo. More than ninety percent of riparian areas in the West have been eliminated by flood control and irrigation projects, so the vegetation along the ditches becomes even more important. Desert riparian areas like the *acequias* provide breeding habitat for over sixty percent of tropical migratory birds; eighty percent of local wild animals use them during some portion of their lives.

I was dismayed to see a mound of dead willows four feet high, the ends white and sharp, cut by a beaver's wide teeth. One of our tenants, Rick, mentioned that he had pulled willows out of the ditch with a hoe until the end of September. "I left the hoe up there one night," he said with a laugh. "In the morning they had woven it into their dam."

Where the gas pipe crossed the ditch, a young cottonwood had grown around it, almost engulfing it. The pipe wasn't in any immediate danger, but something ought to be done about it.

That evening I called Armando. His voice was deep, his tone abrupt, as if he were about to fly out the door. I felt timid. "I live in the first house at the top of the *acequia*."

"I thought that place was sold."

"No. I'm . . ."

"You're Aaron Levy's wife."

"I'm Phaedra Greenwood and I'm home now. I have to put in a headgate."

"You can't."

My voice rose. "I have water rights. The ditch association yanked our headgate."

"It was leaking."

"How am I supposed to irrigate?"

His voice rose, too. "We can't shut down the ditch for even one day. I have animals that depend on that water. You're going to have to wait until fall."

Now I was miffed—and a little paranoid. When were these three cultures—Anglo, Indian and Hispano—going to learn to work together?

The next day as I was washing dishes something large and noisy thrummed past the window. I ran to the back door. A four-wheeler. Probably one of those kids from the village. I'd catch him on his way out.

When I heard him coming back ten minutes later, I popped out the door and stood in the middle of the driveway. The figure on the ATV grew larger and larger—a man, not a boy. I held up one hand and he stopped. The golden-brown eyes and heavy, sober face seemed vaguely familiar.

I waved my dishtowel. "Hi. I'd rather you didn't drive back there unless you have ditch business. This is private property. But you're welcome to park your bike by the outhouse and walk."

His scowl deepened. "I'm Armando Abeyta."

I gulped. I wasn't ready to go head-on with Armando. I held out my hand. "I'm Phaedra."

"I know who you are. We have ditch work to do up in the canyon. We're bringing in some heavy equipment next week."

"That's okay. I'm just trying to discourage traffic."

"The ditch has the right of way."

"I know."

He gave me a narrow-eyed look and pointed to the line of cottonwoods that had been growing along the ditch behind my house for the past twenty years, shielding me from the blast of summer heat.

He watched my face. "All those trees should be cut down," he said. "We shouldn't have let them grow in the first place."

"Okay."

"It's a lotta work, though," he grumbled. He tightened his grip on the handle of his ATV and revved the engine. "I've been trying for months to get the gas company to come out here and cut that tree behind your house that's growing around the pipe. It's right in your back yard. I should think you'd worry."

If I placated him with one tree maybe he'd spare the rest. "I'll give them a call."

His tone was solemn. "Everyone who uses the water should help with the ditch. We've got to work together in this community."

"You've got that right."

He pointed to the mound of willows on the bank of the ditch. "Those beavers were really a pest last summer. I was up here every day pulling out their dams. They're on your property. You should do it."

"I won't let the beavers come back."

His eyes widened. "You promise?"

"I promise."

"You can give me a call if you need help."

"I will."

I called the gas company. Two days later they sent a couple of bigwigs out to "assess the danger." They agreed that the tree should be cut. A week later, two men appeared in a white company truck. They dropped their jackets on the ground and went right to work. "Do you want the branches?" one asked.

"No. I've got plenty of kindling around, but I'd like the logs."

The heavy-set one grinned. "I was going to take them if you didn't want them. Cottonwood burns pretty clean. But don't let those logs sit too long. Once they dry up they're too tough to split."

They felled the tree, cut the trunk into stove-sized pieces, took away the branches and left me the logs. Two points for me.

I called the number Eloy had left and offered him the wood. He came by in the afternoon and I helped him load the logs into the back of his pickup.

I pulled off my gloves. "Armando said they were doing some construction work up in the canyon today. Maybe they'll shut the ditch down?"

"No, they're just adding some rocks at the headgate."

Ten minutes later Armando bumbled up in his old truck followed by a truck towing a backhoe. He idled it and sat watching us. "I see you got that tree cut down."

"I called the gas company."

"Better split those logs before they get too dry."

Eloy thrust out his chin. "There isn't a log that I can't split."

Armando gave him a look of disgust and got out of his truck to supervise the unloading of the backhoe.

The wind picked up in the afternoon; soot-black clouds rolled in from the west and forks of lightning danced from cloud to cloud. I shut down my computer and dashed out to grab the sheets off the line and close the car windows. Birds darted across the sky. Thunder boomed overhead and the wind lashed my cheeks. I fled into the house as torrents of rain let loose. A few minutes later a fury of hail leapt and sizzled on the ground and drummed on the tin roof. Streams of water poured down the windows; every place the roof had ever leaked in the past twenty years was leaking now. I ran from room to room with bowls and pans.

Ten minutes later it was over. I stood under the *portal* shivering, my breath coming out in puffs. The ground was white with hail four inches deep and torrents of muddy water cut new channels in the driveway. My bare feet were bright red as I knelt and dug the hail out from around my pansies. They were miraculously intact, but my vegetable garden was destroyed.

Later I learned this was the worst hailstorm in eighty years but only this end of the valley had been battered—which didn't make me feel any better.

Armando drove up, got out of his truck, hitched up his pants and strolled over. "We have to shut the ditch down for the rest of the day. That storm collapsed the bank back in the canyon. If you can get Eloy over here to bury your pipe, we probably won't have the water back on until noon tomorrow."

"I'll give him a call."

He nodded. "What's happening with the beaver dams up here?"

I showed him the one behind the house. "I'm about one jump ahead of them."

"They're down at my end, too. Do you have a gun?"

"I have a .22, but they're nocturnal."

"They're easy to see in the moonlight swimming up and down."

"I think it would be a shame to shoot them."

He was silent a moment. "Maybe you could put a radio up there at night. The noise would keep them away."

"I don't have an extension cord that long, but I'll try a lantern."

He peered over my shoulder at the ruin of my lettuce. "Nice little garden you have there."

I wanted to spread out my arms and hide it. "It was better before the hail."

The corner of his mouth twitched up in a smile. "So was mine."

Eloy dug out the side of the ditch, installed the culvert, and we filled in the trench together. At dusk I placed kerosene lanterns on flat stones at the edge of the ditch. That slowed the beavers down for about a week until one of the lanterns was stolen. I kept the other one going until I had used up all my kerosene.

"Kerosene is too expensive," I told Armando over the phone. "And they're getting ahead of me."

The next day he came over with his two sons. The oldest, Gabe, was a burly teenager with a black mop of hair. The other boy, about five, stood watching as they brought hoes and rakes. I kicked off my sneakers and plunged into the ditch with Gabe; together we struggled to undo the beavers' work.

Armando leaned on his rake as he caught his breath. "It's time to call the Game and Fish Department."

"What will they do?"

"Get rid of them."

"Do they have live traps?"

"They're not as efficient." He rubbed his chin. "We don't like to kill things, but sometimes you have to."

I searched his face. "Maybe they could just take the beavers somewhere else."

He nodded. "Maybe."

Aaron called to tell me some guy from Taos who heard we were breaking up has called twice to ask if Aaron and I are interested in selling the whole property. To my surprise, Aaron said no. "I'm not ready to break that tie with family and home."

I sighed with relief.

"Rachel wants to come home for awhile," he continued. "She said she'll take the bus."

"I'll drive up to Walsenberg to meet her."

Rachel looked tall, graceful, and old for her age as she stepped off the bus in Walsenberg. She was wearing clean blue jeans and a white blouse. We chatted non-stop all the way home, but she fell silent as we pulled up in the driveway. Neither of us made a move to get out. She stared at the windows. "The house is awake."

I smiled. "Let's go in."

She stood in the living room, turning around slowly, noticing the red and black Navajo rugs on the floor, the Indian pots on the mantle over the adobe fireplace. "It looks just like it did when we lived here. You've done a great job, Mom."

I smiled and she gave me a hug. I followed her into her room. "Except for the curtains, everything is the same," she said, turning to me. "I remember sitting on that window sill watching Dad and Brian setting off fireworks in the yard."

"You wouldn't go out."

"It scared the hell out of me."

We both laughed. She inspected the molding on the hall side of the door and found her mark in the middle. "Measure me now, Mama," she said, standing against the board. "How tall am I now?"

For the next few days I drank from my daughter's nurturing energy with joy and gratitude. We fixed meals together, watched videos, went tubing in the Rio Grande. She was studying Spanish and labeled everything in the house. A piece of tape on the door said, *"Puerta."* I smiled at the quizzical look on Armando's face as I answered his knock. "¡*Hola!*" I said. "I know. It's time to call the Game and Fish Department again."

A few days later a shiny black truck pulled up in the driveway. A tall, young man with ruddy cheeks climbed out. Chuck Dunston was about thirty, blond and handsome. I walked up to the ditch with him and showed him the dams. The beavers had cut through half a cottonwood about eight inches in diameter. "I could put some chicken wire around that," he said.

"It's too late for that one. It's the ditch that's at stake here. The beavers are really making pests of themselves."

He nodded. "But if they fell this tree it will be too heavy to move. Then they'll really have you stumped."

I laughed at the unintentional pun, but he didn't crack a smile. He touched the butt of his gun in the black leather holster. "I could shoot them if you want."

I shook my head. "Can't we set some live traps and take them out of here?"

"I have a few places I could use some live beavers. I'll bring the trap and set it for you."

Rachel and Yona had been sunbathing on the trampoline. Yona was slender, with generous breasts and a wild mass of chestnut curls. Rachel was wearing sunglasses and a yellow tube dress that clung to her curves. Her hair was tucked up with a few strands drooping around her ears. They were strolling toward the house, arms around each other.

I watched out the door as Chuck climbed out of his truck. This time he was in uniform, a pressed blue shirt with a silver badge, black creased pants and shiny black shoes. He banged the truck door and marched up to Rachel and Yona. "I'm here to take care of your beavers, ma'am."

Rachel raised one corner of her sunglasses and smiled. "Oh, really? How nice of you."

He forced down a smile. "Sorry about that," he muttered. His face was still pink when he knocked at the door to tell me he had the live trap. It looked like a wire waffle iron. He showed me how to set it, what it took to spring the trigger. "You want to keep your pets away. When it snaps, it really hurts. We hope the beaver will swim into the middle of it. But if he gets caught and the water rises, he could drown. I need you to check it for me because it's hard to get by every day."

"I will."

I thought a beaver would have to be really dumb to swim into that. Chuck and I waded up the ditch until he found "beaver activity," holes in the banks, one on top and one in the side. "In the daytime the beavers live in the banks," he said.

Their holes are large; when they back up the water with their dams, it pours out through the holes into my fields. Illegal irrigation.

Go somewhere else, beavers. Time to leave. It isn't safe here anymore.

Chuck set the trap with a fresh-cut willow branch in the middle for bait. He weighted the bottom of the cage with a large rock and jammed some sticks into the bottom of the ditch in an "X" to hold the trap in place.

I felt uneasy about the waiting trap. I checked it every morning for the next three days. The beavers worked around it. The wilting branch didn't seem to tempt them. Why should it? They had so much loose stuff already cut.

On the fourth day I found the trap snapped with a branch stuck in it. The next time I pulled out a beaver dam I noticed that they were jamming sticks into the bottom of the ditch using an "X" to hold the branches in place.

Eloy came by one day to tell me that Armando said I could water my orchard on Saturday. "I said, 'Hey, her orchard is a garden, isn't it? Why can't she water on garden day with everybody else?'"

I thanked him and gave him a hug. Next spring I'd plant new

trees, more apricots and plums, maybe even cherries.

On Saturday when I walked up to the ditch, the water was too low to irrigate. But a beaver dam a few yards below my pipe had backed up the water into a pool three feet deep. I uncapped the pipe and watched the water trickle into my orchard. "Thanks, beavers," I said. "Some days you do me a favor, and some days I do you one. But you really ought to leave now—go back to the mountains."

To celebrate Yona's nineteenth birthday, she and Rachel and I climbed up to the petroglyph rock in the moonlight. In the canyon below, the moon sparkled on the black water of the Rio Hondo. The soft summer wind carried the scents and sounds of the desert, a hoot owl in the distance, the sudden yipping of a coyote.

Yona rose and stretched, hands circling above her head. She removed her hair tie and shook out her curls. "I want us to take off our clothes and dance to the land," she said, sliding out of her jeans.

That evening in the moonlight three naked graces hummed, pranced and swayed to the primal rhythms of the stones and stars.

I glanced out the window one morning and saw one of the young cottonwoods lying in the field near the *rio*. A day or two later, the beavers felled another one. When I went down to the river to inspect the damage, I counted five young trees freshly cut. And they had the nerve to chew six inches into my sacred swing tree. The apple trees would be next.

I went out, bought a roll of chicken wire and spent four hours bent over, measuring and cutting wire on the ground. I wired fifty trees on the property and pulled the muscles in my back so badly that they would never heal.

A couple of nights later when I was late coming home from town I heard water gurgling through a hole in the side of the ditch behind the house. By flashlight I discovered that my driveway was flooded and the leach field for my septic tank was under six inches of water.

"God damn it!" I ran back to the house to get my rake. The toilets and sinks would back up. I'd have to get someone out here to pump out the tank—for how much? A hundred? I stumbled up to the ditch, jumped in, wrenched the branches out and tossed them up on the bank.

In the morning I called the Game and Fish Department. I was sitting on a stone when Armando drove across the bridge in his creaky, green pickup. He stopped and rolled down the window.

I nodded hello. "I was waiting for someone, but you're not him."

"Too bad."

"Those beavers have gotten the best of me."

"Me too. I've been fighting them down at my end. I thought they had moved down there."

"They're using stones up here—big ones. They pile them on top of the willows."

"At the other end where the willows run out they're cutting sagebrush and cedar."

"You gave me enough rope to hang myself."

We were silent a moment, eye to eye. He grinned. I smiled. He threw up his hands. "Thanks for trying."

"Thanks for helping me."

Another battered pickup rolled past. I followed it to the orchard. Out climbed a bearded fellow in a cap, wearing suspenders and hip boots. "My name is Darwin McHand," he said, and spelled his last name. "I'm working with the Game and Fish Department. I trap beaver."

"Dead?"

"It's more efficient." He held up his trap. "It's really a very humane one. It snaps shut on their spine, knocks them out and then they drown. Beavers are dirty. They shit in the water and spread giardia. They don't know the ditch water is temporary."

"We should put up a sign. Where are you going to set your trap?"

He waved his hand. "Back in the canyon. You won't even see it."

After he left I walked back up in the canyon looking for "beaver sign." I found a hole in the top of the ditch and another one below it on the inside. Around the trunk of an alder tree I noticed the gleam of a chain that held the trap in place. There were holes like this all along the bank. Why here?

The next day the truck came back. I hurried down to the orchard. Four people got out: Darwin, then a slender woman in jeans, and two young boys in camouflage suits. The woman was pretty, with dark hair pulled back in a barrette, a thin face and rosy cheeks.

I said, "I want to see if you caught anything."

Darwin adjusted his suspenders. "I'll stop by your house on the way out. I'll be back in about an hour. My family and I are going for a walk in the canyon."

The woman was silent. She and Darwin turned their backs, joined hands and walked off, with the children hopping along behind. In less than an hour I heard the truck and hurried to the door. Darwin rolled down his window and jerked his thumb toward the back. On a pile of wood lay a granddaddy beaver, at least forty pounds.

"I'll make good use of the skin," he said, "get maybe sixty or seventy dollars for it. I'll feed the meat to the dogs."

I had never seen a beaver up close. The tail wasn't as big as I imagined. It crossed my mind to grab my camera and take a picture—Darwin in his cap and checked flannel shirt craning his neck out the window, the beaver splayed out in back.

He scratched under his beard. "I caught him going in. The

jaws snapped him right behind the head. I doubt he ever felt a thing. He was lying out flat in the water, just like that. I'll be back in a few days to see if there are any more, but I suspect it's just that one. He cut off from the main bunch and has been living like a hermit. When they're big like that, they travel. They'll build a series of dams up and down the line."

I stared at the beaver's dark length, his rumpled fur. Hard to believe it was just this one animal I had been fighting all summer.

It wasn't, of course. I was fighting a force of nature. Next summer they'd be back.

Beside the Rio Hondo

No day is entirely lost if I can find time to go down to the swing. I follow the steep path that plunges down the hill in front of the house, meanders across the field and joins with a grassy path that has been made by the feet of local fishermen and wandering children.

The log I clamber over at the edge of the field was once my favorite tree, a narrow-leafed cottonwood with a six-foot girth and silvery bark like braided hemp. During my first decade in Arroyo Hondo I watched our giant cottonwood die from the top down, the tips of its branches slowly turning white. I had never lived in one place long enough to mourn the passing of an old tree.

To keep it from falling on the Cohns' fence across the river, we had our gnarled giant cut down. Here it lies, bark sliding off in wide slabs, massive trunk laced with vines of Apache plume, a home for rabbits and squirrels. I wanted to give a section of the trunk to Red Shirt at Taos Pueblo to make a drum, but Red Shirt has crossed over, too. I will use the scattered bark and branches for kindling to honor this old tree every time I light a fire.

At this end of the valley most of the big trees are dying. People speak of them as "ancient" but they don't live much longer than we do. They can only re-seed during a brief two weeks in the spring, which is cleverly timed with the runoff. For the seeds to sprout, the river has to flood the banks, but that hasn't happened for a number of years. With El Niño and global warming, we have long periods of drought, then fire.

Old-timers say that during spring runoff the river was high, fast and dangerous. They had to make sure the children didn't go near it; people drowned. Winters were colder, with deep snow. Some say that when the Hondo froze over they cut huge blocks of ice and stored them in sawdust for summer refrigeration. Others say they used ice blocks cut from lakes in Colorado.

Hollyhock

The grassy path curves down the bank through a young cottonwood grove. My view is hidden for a few moments by a dark sentinel, a young tree with a tangle of dead branches around the trunk. The shimmer of water beyond heightens the sense of mystery.

As I round the sentinel tree the bank opens to the horizontal rush of the river. The eye is greeted by a vault of shadowed space defined at the top by the muscular curve of a cottonwood bough. Rooted too close together, two giant trees bend away from each other and reach across the stream. In dappled play of sunlight and water, blue nylon ropes—lines of color borrowed from the sky—hang down thirty feet from the arched branch to support an unpainted board.

Before me in the middle of the stream is a flat slab of basalt—my centering place. In autumn when the sun shines through the yellow leaves, it's the only place for me.

In my early teens I began to seek comfort in nature. Whenever I was depressed, discouraged or in pain, I followed narrow paths that ran downhill to water, sought out still black pools in the woods, brisk lakes, deep rivers, lively creeks. Beside the water I prayed for patience and courage and strength and gave thanks for the beauty of life.

I sit on the grassy bank of the Rio Hondo and watch patterns in the surface of the water, ripples above the big rock, a rush and thrust of rills, then the clean still pool below, clear to the bottom, sandy and green. Sunlight illuminates the alder trees and my golden dog sitting motionless on the stone watching the currents.

Years ago, with a woman friend, I followed the Rio Hondo back to its source at Williams Lake ten thousand feet up the mountain. I saw how the braided streams converge in Taos Ski Valley, then rush down the mountain through crystalline bedrock, leaping over boulders, sliding under fallen spruce trees, hurrying between high crags as the creek descends for two thousand feet along the paved highway.

The Hondo grows more placid as it glides through the village of Valdez, murmuring between big cottonwoods. Isolated by steep hillsides, the valley floor is half a mile wide, scattered with trailers and old adobes. Over succeeding generations the land has been divided into narrow ribbons so that each family can have access to water. "Downtown" consists of a church, a post office, a bar and an abandoned *morada* where the *Los Hermanos de Penitentes*, also called the Brothers of Light, performed their secret rites. So far Valdez has successfully resisted the encroachment of condos and other commercial ventures in a heartfelt attempt to preserve the water and a rural way of life. In the seventies the "condo wars" sparked the revival of an old tradition. On *Día de San Antonio*, the feast day of St. Anthony, patron saint of the San Antonio Mission, the people of Valdez attend mass, then process to the bridge to bless the waters of the Rio Hondo.

At the end of Valdez the water returns from the *acequias* to the Rio Hondo, which cuts through the high cliffs of Cañoncito for about a mile. In the heart of the canyon the stream is again diverted into ditches that flank both sides of the Hondo valley. The diminished Rio Hondo crosses under State Highway 522 and snakes down through lower Hondo past the elementary school and the Varellas' pastures where they keep a couple of glossy horses and a small flock of sheep. At the end of the valley the ditches return about sixty percent of the water to the *rio*.

The canyon walls grow steep as the stream slices through volcanic basalt on its final descent to the Rio Grande. The rushing waters fill trout pools and burble past rock climbers as they rappel down the steep cliffs on their nylon ropes.

By the time the Rio Hondo joins the shallow waters of the Rio Grande at the John Dunn Bridge, this high mountain stream has traveled seventeen miles, through fifteen *acequias*, and watered the livestock, gardens, orchards and fields of all the *parciantes* in both valleys. In the spring doctors and former Wall Street executives, landowners who have water rights, work shoulder-to-shoulder with Spanish-speaking farmers and ranchers to maintain the *acequias*.

When I first came to the Hondo house, there was no running water except in the summer when we pumped water from the ditch behind the house to the kitchen sink. We used an outhouse and bathed outside under a camp shower hung from a *viga* at the back of the house. Showering outdoors in the sunlight with the breeze teasing your backside, washing off soap bubbles through rainbows of spray, is an exotic experience.

In winter we trudged down the hill to the Rio Hondo to fill our buckets from a hole Aaron had dug in the streambed close to the bridge. I learned how to make every drop of water go three times: I used the dishwater to mop the floor and scrub the stove, the rinse water to water the plants.

Neither of us minded the outhouse, and swimming in the Rio Grande was a great way to bathe in the summer, but in winter we longed for a real bathtub and a hot shower. To drill a well and install plumbing would have cost about five thousand dollars. The bathroom would have to wait.

For drinking water we drove through Taos to Cañon and filled up our five-gallon jerry cans from a hillside spring. The cold mountain water from *La Vinateria* was the best-tasting water anywhere. But I never imagined I'd be hauling drinking water for the next thirty years. Eventually we put in a bathroom. Water comes from seepage that pours into a culvert buried upright in the bank six feet from the river. It's okay for dishes and bathing, but we can't drink it. Twice a year I lower myself into it and fish out the crickets and dead mice.

I clutch the nylon ropes of the swing, back up to the boulder, and hop on the broad seat. The wind whirrs against the ropes as I arc through curved space twenty feet above the river. The ssshhh of the water rushes my ears as I approach and fades as I swoop back. The air is cool above the stream, warmer on the hillside. The briar patch gives off the fragrance of wild roses. Their blossoms are like delicate palms lifted to the sky.

When my momentum slows, I throw my head back, tuck my legs under and spin, spotting on the web of branches where three cottonwoods meet. Swinging backward toward the stream, I catch sight of the small adobe on the hill with the blue window frames. For a moment I enter some disembodied future when I have lost my identity, but see the house with my heart, as in a dream. Oh yes, I remember. I loved that place!

Back on solid ground, I wander over to the massive trunk of the swingtree, which is wider than my arms can stretch. I thank the old cottonwood for growing here and give its shaggy trunk a hug. Then I climb onto the altar of the broad, flat rock in the center of the stream. The water that swirls past its tip is glassy green, like a marble. Spring run-off has scoured the bottom clean; the stones are black, white, yellow, buff and lavender. A sand bar has gathered on the downstream side—sweeping curves echoed by wave patterns in lines of light.

I watch the fluctuating design. For years I have crouched under bridges, waded upstream, lain on the bank studying the hieroglyphics of water. The patterns change and change, but the gracefully balanced shapes remain the same.

Water spirals through embryos, tissues and bones, and shapes every living thing. You don't have to be a scientist to understand this. At an anti-nuclear rally I paused in the wings offstage to listen to an elder from Taos Pueblo speak to the crowd. "We love that big mountain standing there," Paul Bernal said. "We love that water coming through the Pueblo. That water comes from the source, at the head, and that source is not made by human beings. It's made by God. God has struggled to give us this life. Water is what makes us look like what we are today. That mountain is sacred. The Indian feels that water is very sacred. Without clean water, we cannot survive."

This constant flow of life evokes an invisible meaning. Cycles of geological time revolve from sea to mountain to sea, swirling clouds driven by the cosmic engine of sun and wind, melting glaciers and shifting continents that reduce human civilization to an afterthought.

Gazing upstream, I notice pools of dark algae near the banks. Still too many nutrients in the stream. I began to notice a change in the Rio Hondo in 1974 when I went down to fill my buckets. The rocks looked all the same—an ugly shade of pea green—with sludgy-looking creatures clung to them. The *rio* was dying before my eyes.

We needed the water, and it had to be clean. That was the bottom line, but I had no idea what I was getting into the day I met Connie Zamora. A petite woman with short, black hair and owl-like glasses, she looked stranded behind her big desk. She shook my hand in a firm grip and looked me square in the eyes. "I've seen you at the Hondo post office. Where do you live?"

"Below the gas line, at the top of the Atalaya."

She sized me up. "Do you work?"

"No." Taking care of a house, husband and two children is not considered work.

"Do you have time to circulate some petitions?" She hurried on before I could answer. "The Ski Valley is applying for federal money to build a big new sewage treatment plant so they can expand their facilities. The old plant would work, but they've neglected it so they can claim it isn't big enough."

"Don't you think it would be better if someone Spanish did it?"

"I don't think it matters. We all depend on the water."

She laid her glasses on the desk and tried to smooth away the frown lines between her eyes. "In the old days the river was much more a part of our daily lives. People worked harder, but they pulled together back then. One of my favorite things as a child was wool washing. Every spring we carried the mattresses outside, opened them up and pulled out the wool. We built fires to get the water hot and scrubbed the wool in big tubs beside the river. We rinsed it in cold water and lay it on the grass to dry. Then it had to be turned over. We all did it together, out there in the sun on a beautiful spring day, chatting and having a picnic." She bit her lower lip. Her teeth were very white. "Those days are gone," she said, "but the Rio Hondo is still flowing through our lives."

When I got home I typed up some petitions. I set out in the heat of the afternoon with both kids in the back seat of the car in a confusion of melting crayons and torn coloring books. I promised them Popsicles if they didn't fight as I made my way door to door from one end of the valley to the other.

What struck me afterward was how different the Hispanos were from each other. Some were Republicans, some Democrats, some farmers and some laborers at the Moly Mine. Some were uneducated; others were well off, sophisticated and informed.

In 1878, somewhere in this valley, Cleofas Martínez was born and raised in a seventeen-room house, the daughter of a wealthy, educated family. After she married and became Cleofas Martínez Jaramillo, she founded the Sociedad Folklórica and wrote and published three books. One was *Romance of a Little Village Girl* in which she wrote about her idyllic childhood beside the "crystalline waters" of the Rio Hondo: "In this little valley of the Rio Hondo River . . . hemmed in by high mountains, and hills, sheltered from the contamination of the outside world, the inhabitants lived peacefully, preserving the customs and traditions of their ancestors. . . . Everyone seemed happy in those days. The peace that lay over the land imparted to its inhabitants satisfactions and contentment. How could it be otherwise, living according to God's laws and close to the good earth and the natural beauties of nature?"

In the upper valley everyone was bilingual, but at the lower end I had to resort to *"Por el río, la agua . . . por favor. Muchas gracias."* At almost every house they listened politely, passed the petition around and everyone in the family signed.

"We just want to live like a human being," said Ignacio Montoya, drawing himself up to his full height, stroking his silver belt buckle with his thumb. "If we let the river get too bad, it's our children that's going to suffer. When I was a boy, we all drank out of that river. That's all there was. We used to eat the fish, but now they're all slimy."

Consuelo Baca was eighty-one years old, with high cheekbones and sculpted white hair that rose two inches above her head. She offered me a seat and looked over my petition.

"I've lived here all my life," she said, eyeing me over her glasses. "I remember when Taos Ski Valley was called Twining. When I was a girl we used to drive up the mountain in a wagon to cut wood. It took all day. There was nothing up there but the old turquoise mine. But now—you talk about pollution—there wasn't any pollution until you people started coming here."

"The cities are smog-bound, not good places to raise children."

"I understand," she said, "but I was here first."

Our eyes met and neither of us spoke for a moment. A flicker of a smile hovered around her mouth. "How many children do you have?"

"Two. They're in the car."

Her voice softened. "I have nine grandchildren."

"That must be wonderful."

"They're here every day." She sighed. "Well, I'll sign this, just because you care enough to bring it around. But I don't think it will make any difference."

Connie and I met at the school cafeteria. With a core group of a dozen people we formed the Committee To Save the Rio Hondo (CTSRH). When Andrés Martínez stood up to speak, everyone in the room fell silent. He was a small, well-made man in his seventies with a brown weathered face, a wavy mass of white hair and a gleam in his blue eyes. For years he had worked with the *acequia* associations in Taos. Local author John Nichols called him one of the "keepers of the flame."

"Have courage," he said. "Be strong and stick up for your rights."

I left my quiet, sunny niche to serve for five years as secretary and the legs of the Committee to Save the Rio Hondo. I arrived at my first Environmental Protection Agency (EPA) hearing prepared to do a little show and tell with my chipped enamel bucket and some slimy stones I had fished out of the river. The press loved it; the opposition hated it. The battle was on.

The fight to save the Rio Hondo was the most hotly-fought and widely-publicized political struggle in Taos County. On one side were the economic powers, the lodgers and restaurateurs, the ski industry and everyone in town who benefited from skier traffic. They were quick to point out that it was the skiers who kept Taos alive in the winter. "We create jobs," said a Ski Valley spokesman.

On the other side were those feisty, dark-skinned, downstream users. One of them wrote a letter to the editor of *The Taos News* saying that they didn't want those demeaning jobs wiping toilets for minimum wage.

Over the next five years we polarized the whole town, roused the rabble and united the ditch associations with the environmentalists. We timed our first demonstration up at Taos Ski Valley to block the morning rush of skiers who were racing to get up on the slopes. A hundred dusty cars and battered pickups crawled in a long line up the mountain. Taos Ski Valley had never seen such a rag-tag caravan; one of the vehicles caught fire and had to pull over.

At the bridge we tied on our black armbands and unloaded a black coffin that bore a sign, "*El Río Está Muerto*," the river is dead. We marched to the bridge and performed a mock funeral, then lined up on both sides. Skiers had to run the gauntlet as we chanted, "Ski, don't flush! Ski, don't flush!" We handed out flyers about pollution and waved our placards that said crude things like, "We don't fish in your toilet. Don't pee in our river." Or, more simply, "Ski, don't pee!"

The skiers in their bright polyester suits eyed us like skittish horses as they trotted across the bridge. The Ski Valley officials hated it. The state police monitored us and the media videotaped the whole thing.

The problem was that all the plant wastewater had to be returned to the river to meet the demand of downstream users. We didn't want gallons of chlorine or other chemicals mixed with our irrigation and household water.

For years we worked with officials from Taos Ski Valley on two different citizens' advisory committees until we mutually agreed on a treatment plant that purified wastewater by ultraviolet light. It was important that we were included in the decision-making process, that our voices were heard. Working with the Forest Service, we struggled with every detail of the Ski Valley's proposed expansion, from the size of the parking lot to the type of sand for snowy roads and a possible shuttle service. We lost a few battles and won a few concessions. I'd like to say that we saved the Rio Hondo, but now the Village of Taos Ski Valley is planning to build a two-hundred-thousand gallon per day plant to accommodate future development. The State of New Mexico Environment Department approved the project, saying that the expansion will have no significant impact on the river. It might be a good idea to hook up old condos to the plant instead of polluting the groundwater with septic tanks, but construction, increased traffic and new and improved roads, both upstream and down, are bound to have a significant impact on the river, especially in years of drought.

When Brian was about seven, the village children often came to the swing. It didn't take the boys long to figure out how to remove the seat so they could swing on one rope. I was annoyed because they rarely put the seat back on, or they got it crooked.

One afternoon Brian recognized some of the boys from school and went down to play. Ten minutes later he came panting back to the house, his face bright red, cheeks wet with tears. They refused to let him on the swing. He said the oldest boy punched him in the stomach. I started down the hill but when they saw me coming they ran like shaggy ponies across the field.

The next day when I went down to the swing, I found one of the ropes cut about four feet above the ground and a garter snake impaled on the line. The sight of the snake's slack body made me shudder as if they had put a curse on the swing. With the rope cut, I no longer had the option of a swing seat. A chill passed through me, then a wave of sadness.

A couple of days later we had an outdoor party. Brian and his friends were swinging on the remaining rope while I sat on the other side of the tree playing my guitar. A cry from Brian brought me to my feet. He was lying on the ground with his arm bent backward at the wrist like a snapped branch.

He was seven years old and weighed almost sixty pounds but I scooped him up in my arms, scrambled up the steep hill, jumped in the car and screamed for Aaron to drive us to the hospital. Two hours later, after pain shots, X-rays and a temporary cast, Dr. Al Rosen smiled at me. "Well, how does it feel to be the mother of a boy with a broken arm?"

"Terrible!"

Over the next year the swing ropes grew shorter and shorter until they were so high above our heads we couldn't reach them. Maybe the hemp shrank in the sun and the magpies took the pieces away for their nests.

For the born-again swing I chose nylon rope so I wouldn't have to worry about it growing frayed. A friend of mine tied a rock to a string and the other end of the string to the rope, then tossed the rock over the branch and pulled the rope through its own noose. At the top it was secured with three feet of chain.

I decided not to paint the seat but claimed my territory by scratching with a Bic pen: "Welcome to my favorite spot where I come to be quiet and cool, to be happy and sad, to listen to the river and be one with the wind. Trespassers will be forgiven, but please be gentle with yourselves, and each other and my swing!" I drew a flower and signed, "Phaedra Greenwood—Up on The Hill."

This morning the gas man paused at my door and smiled down at the swing. "Is that yours?"

I nodded.

His bronze face broke in a grin. "I used to come here when I was a kid. It was like a park."

I watched the children from the village drift back to the swing. When their cries reached a certain pitch, I made myself conspicuous watering the flowers.

In the afternoon the shrill sound of little girls drew me to the door. In the field below a young woman headed home carrying her toddler piggyback. Two older girls lingered behind. I went down to ask their names. The one with braids and a missing front tooth hesitated as she reached for the swing rope. "Is it okay?"

"Yes, but be careful. If anyone gets hurt, I'll have to take it down. And when you leave, take your gum wrappers."

"We will," she promised, watching me with round, brown eyes. "My mother told me about this swing. She said she used to come and play on it when she was a little girl."

On a warm Sunday evening a boy and a girl strolled across the field holding hands. She was wearing a white dress. "I know where you're headed," I said as they disappeared behind the thicket of small cottonwoods. A few moments later they swung out over the river, side by side on the weathered wooden seat.

I hope the swing tree lives long enough for my grandchildren to enjoy it—if I have any—to be part of their childhood memories. I have a fantasy that when the old tree dies and the swing branch falls, my days beside the Rio Hondo will be over, too. But like Faustus, some part of me may still drift through spring shadows seeking the lost magic in the golden ripples of the Rio Hondo.

Mud and Romance

*T*oday as I rode my bike past the Cohns' house I noticed a man burning weeds with a flame-thrower. His expression was fierce. He wore a red bandanna tied around his forehead; sweat ran down his dark, handsome face. Reynaldo García. He must be forty now. I hadn't seen him in years, though I often saw him quoted in the paper. He had been the youngest member of the Committee to Save the Rio Hondo and was now their spokesman. From what I read in the paper he was heavily involved in fighting the proposed jet extension for the airport. I pulled over.

"Hi."

He glanced up. "Hi."

I grinned. "Is that it? Just `Hi'?"

He stared at me across the fence.

I waved. "It's me, Phaedra."

He nodded, chagrined.

I told him I'd help the Committee catch up on the paperwork. He told me Taos Ski Valley was going to use the big lift this summer when the Environmental Impact Statement (EIS) said they were supposed to remove it. "The Forest Service supervisor is a shit—worse than the last one," he said.

"And the Ski Valley never lets up." I laughed. "Don't get me mad all over again. I just got home." I told him I'd like to help plaster the church when they got around to it.

He pulled off one glove and wiped his forehead. "Just stop by when you see us working." I'd forgotten his strong Spanish accent. The oldest child in a large family, Reynaldo has lived all his life in the village. I met his father at a party once—a large, homely man with warm, brown eyes who played guitar with great skill while we sang traditional Spanish songs. I had learned a few of these wonderful songs with my children when I served as an aide at the Arroyo Hondo elementary school.

"How's Debra?" I asked. I had an image of her—a willowy Anglo woman with long, blonde hair. The last I heard they were living together.

"We split up."

"I'm sorry," I said, my heart rising. "Aaron and I broke up, too."

"How come?"

I shrugged. "He never wanted to take the scenic route."

He smiled, showing even white teeth. I was tempted to bring him a cold Mt. Dew from Herb's, but I didn't. Don't court him, I told myself. Don't ask him over to dinner. This guy is shy. The best way to reconnect is by working together. And don't go off on fantasy flights about him either. I pedaled on down the road humming, "Spanish is a loving tongue . . ."

Today I rode my bike past the church and saw Lorenzo Ortiz and Archie Trujillo chopping straw, while Larry Herrera mixed a tub of mud with a hoe. Lorenzo is sturdy and handsome, with light brown hair. He was a kid when I left. Archie is a friendly giant with a long, black ponytail. Herrera stretched his back and met my hello with a shy smile. I asked if they needed help.

Archie grinned, "Sure." I didn't dare ask if Reynaldo would be around. I would plaster to be part of the community, for love of the church.

Nuestra Señora de los Dolores has seen some changes since it was dedicated in 1833. The original design of the Spanish Franciscan friars was a flat roof and huge buttresses on the corners, but around 1916 Father Joseph Giraud launched an extensive remodeling project. The buttresses were removed and a belfry and gabled shingle roof were added. Gothic arches sprang up over the windows and the original bell, supposedly cast in Spain, was replaced by a school bell. But nothing could alter the intrinsic strength and grace of the original structure. Some years later the rotting shingles on the roof were replaced by aluminum sheathing. To help protect the adobe, the walls were hard-plastered. Painted white, they reflected the colors of the day: blue in the morning, yellow at noon and pink in the evening sun. Pink and red hollyhocks lined the walk.

"I liked how it changed colors when it was white," I said.

Archie took a slug of water from a plastic bottle and wiped his mouth. "Cement and adobe are not a marriage made in heaven."

Larry leaned on his hoe, wiped his forehead and regarded me with deep brown eyes. "Adobe needs to breathe, and it can't when it's hard plastered inside and out. The moisture gets trapped under the plaster and the adobe deteriorates."

Archie said, "I'd prefer square windows to the Gothic ones that French priest brought in, but they'll probably stay like they are."

I had read about their restoration efforts in *The Taos News*. In the 1980s Trujillo, Herrera and Ortiz took a tour around Northern New Mexico to look at old *moradas* and churches from Truchas to Abiquiu and Ojo Caliente. "I started learning things about adobe construction that weren't being done anymore," Herrera had said.

Then Trujillo had contacted Cornerstones Community Partnerships, an organization that works with the United States

Chapter of International Council on Monuments and Sites. He asked for technical advice and assistance. Cornerstones' engineers came to Arroyo Hondo, drilled into the adobe and took core samples that showed that moisture was accumulating around the north wall. Several cracks were found. Something had to be done before they lost the whole back wall.

"We never said our elders were wrong," Trujillo explained. "Everyone who has been involved with the church tried to do what they could, with a lot of effort, to maintain this building. But the techniques we found that worked here most were those of our ancestors."

Cornerstones became involved because of the enthusiasm, commitment and diplomacy of these three community leaders. Not everyone agreed on how to fix it, but the Restoration Committee was ready to hold community meetings and explain the process in every last detail, the article said.

In 1990 a volunteer crew pulled the plaster down and locals spent three summers repairing the walls, taking out the adobe rubble until they tied the wall in with the original rock and mud footing. It was a safe procedure because the base of the wall is about four feet thick. They replaced the decayed material with good adobe. For the past two years they had been gradually re-plastering the walls in the traditional New Mexican style, with sand, straw and mud.

I mulled over the gossip I had heard at the post office. "It's taken three years to get the church re-plastered," one disgruntled resident said. "The whole thing has been a fiasco. They removed the cement from around the foundation and the rain is wearing away the bricks. It's just Lorenzo, Archie and Larry. They won't let the old people work because they say they don't know what they're doing, so we don't come around anymore. It was supposed to be a community thing."

I thought they should be grateful they had three solid,

knowledgeable men who were willing to work like slaves for nothing.

I climbed the scaffolding on the west side and worked in the shade while Lorenzo plastered the east wall. Larry and Archie mixed the mud and handed it up to us in white plastic buckets. The adobe was gritty and exuded a dank river-bottom smell. We had barely gotten started when Lorenzo's sister stopped by to say she needed help pulling a pump out of her well. They jumped in her car and took off. Must be nice to have men at your beck and call when you need them.

I plastered until I ran out of mud, then climbed down, helped myself to more half buckets and heaved them up onto the scaffolding. Ironic that I had come to "help" but ended up working alone for about an hour. When I had plastered all of the wall I could reach I decided to take Ocho down to the Rio Grande and go tubing.

It's a shining day, nobody down here in the Gorge except a dark, skinny man with two little girls. When I'm five feet away he drops his shorts and steps into the water. I balance my tube on my head and walk on by.

This time of year the river is low, clear and smooth as silk, a ribbon of light flowing quietly between the cliffs. The water reflects grassy green banks and a mass of yellow coneflowers framed by rosy basalt walls, and in the center, a swatch of turquoise sky. Tiger swallowtails float above the banks and cliff swallows soar back and forth, trailing banners of song. On the other side of the river local fishermen cast their lines for rainbow trout, browns and pike.

Avoiding the poison ivy and eyeing the mint, I follow the rocky trail upstream clambering over shiny black boulders polished by human hands. I'll pick the wild mint to dry for tea; on some bleak winter day as I pour the hot water over the leaves and the sweet, pungent smell rushes into my nose, I'll have this summer day again.

Sitting on a rock, I feel small and alone, dwarfed by these volcanic boulders, the ancient bluffs that stretch toward a clean, blue sky. Geologists say that this area, the Taos Plateau, is "one of the most dynamic and stimulating geologic settings on the planet." It's humbling to realize that the river is following an enormous fissure in the Earth's crust that would be hundreds of feet deeper if the Rio Grande were not back-filling it with boulders and sand. The Rio Grande Rift, one of the few young continental rift valleys in the world, runs six hundred miles down from the San Juans in Colorado and slices New Mexico in half. For the past thirty million years, plate tectonic forces have been tearing the continent apart, inch by inch. The rift is thirty times larger than the Gorge and six times deeper than the Grand Canyon. In the stillness I can feel the inexorable tug of continents straining away in an adagio of eons. On a delta of sand at my feet, the currents have drawn feathered arteries in basalt brown and volcanic black. Here wandering tribes carved their glyphs into the rock faces and made feather shrines.

Eloy says the Rio Grande is the *sangre*, the lifeblood of New Mexico. All streams empty into the big river: Red River ten miles north of us, the Arroyo Seco, the Rio Hondo, the Rio Pueblo, the Rio Lucero, the Rio Fernando, the Rio Grande del Rancho, the Rio Chiquito, and the Rio Embudo thirty miles downstream where the walls of the Gorge dissolve into orchards and vineyards and the muddy water quickens fields of chile and *frijoles*.

This artery of life is also a river of death. Every year it claims a few more hikers and rock climbers. Cars skid off the curves of the highway into the final embrace of the river. Rafters are flipped out into the wild spring runoff. The roadside is littered with crosses decorated with bright plastic flowers. During a storm near Dixon a Trailways bus was smashed by falling boulders and a number of passengers were killed.

The graceful Rio Grande Gorge Bridge draws thousands of tourists every year, and an increasing number of suicides.

Depressed by the turmoil in the world, a young married couple leapt together from the metal railing to the river six hundred and fifty feet below.

The whole community was shocked when a young man was robbed of his truck and clothing, half-strangled and thrown over the bridge to his death.

One summer evening I raced home through the canyon from Española to Taos with a mass of black clouds at my left shoulder. When I reached the safety of the mesa I pulled over to look back. Thunder boomed like Armageddon; bolts of lightning sprang from a black sky. Later I learned that the storm brought down a cascade of boulders that trapped several cars in the canyon overnight.

Here at the John Dunn Bridge a white cross stands on the east bank while behind me a flowered cross for another drowned man is painted on the face of a boulder.

This is the first time I've ever been down to swim in the river alone. It was always a family thing—those hot summer days when we grabbed our sandy tennis shoes with the holes in the toes, stuffed our sagging inner tubes in the trunk and hurried down to the river to play before the afternoon thunderstorms blew in. Aaron loved the river. He was always the first one in.

I gave birth to both babies like this—went down to the river, swam across and back once, and went into labor that night. When Brian was eighteen days old I brought him down to the hot springs close beside the Rio Grande. Lying on his back, naked in the black water with only my hand under his neck, he unfurled like origami, stretched out and lay still. As the last rays of the sun lit the walls of the canyon painting the pool with vibrant reflections, a round silver moon rose in a balance of fullness and opposition.

The ache in my chest hurts so much I want to turn back. But I'm damned if I'll forego tubing even if I have to do it alone. I follow the familiar path upstream lifting the tube high as I pass the spiny cholla. A quarter of a mile upstream I pause on the sandy bank where Aaron and I stole away from the kids to make love. Afterward he dove into the icy green water and came up with a shout: "God! I feel ten years younger."

Tubing in July is a meditation. I wade knee deep into the middle and launch myself belly down across my tube, close my eyes and drift. The only way I can tell if I'm moving at all is by the changing sounds, a side-stream trickling into the river, Ocho splashing along the bank. The canyon wren treats me to a burst of liquid song.

This is as close as I can get to heaven on earth. The white-hot sun bakes my shoulders while the ice green water numbs my legs. Both sensations are so sharp that soon I can hardly tell one from the other. The extremes merge and I hang in the middle, timeless, weightless, ecstatic.

Today I listen with my heart and the river speaks: No need to hurry, no place to go. Everything is here in this moment. You are one with the ever-changing cycles of sun and snowmelt, of flood and drought and rain, one with the bubbling lava below, one with the silence and the chorus. These bones of the earth are passing, but not you. Nothing is moving; all is still.

As the river narrows between two sand spits I paddle into position to catch the quickening current. This was the site of the old bridge where years ago John Dunn drove back and forth across the *rio* from Tres Piedras to Taos to deliver the mail. Here the flow is swift, the water over my head. If I've calculated right, I'll miss the rocky point by a foot and the backflow will swing me in to the beach.

I hike up the bank and tube down twice, then toss my shoes and T-shirt aside. I stand poised on the rocky point, catch a deep breath, plunge into the strong current and swim across with vigorous, measured strokes calculated to bring me to a sloping rock on the other bank. I heave myself up and shake the cold, silver drops from my eyes; my chest expands. I sigh and stretch full length on my back to absorb the sandy warmth of the stone. When the storm rolls in and lightning cracks I'll laugh at the sky: "Oh, let me die floating down the Rio Grande.

I stop by the church on the way home to look for Reynaldo. Archie and Lorenzo are up on the scaffolding. "We're back. Are you going to help?"

I hang on the fence for a minute, feeling sleepy, but let them persuade me. The sun is blazing on the western wall. Archie climbs down to hand me a bucket of mud. I sprinkle the wall and myself with water from a big paintbrush.

Pickups rumble by as we work. The couple next door pounds on their roof while their kids gather apricots in the yard below. Down the road sheep are baaaing—the ram in a distinctly deeper tone. Luis and Pancho putt by on their scooters and wave. The sun burns the backs of my arms. I pause to put on more lotion. "Are there other women who help plaster?"

Lorenzo says, "Loretta Rodríguez. She wears yellow kitchen gloves."

"I like the feel of the mud. Guess I didn't get enough of it when I was a kid." When I've finished that spot I walk around to see if I can learn something from Lorenzo's technique. He slaps on clumps of mud in rows and smears them with the heel of his hand in a slow upward motion, caressing the body of the church as if it were a woman.

"It takes a long time," I say.

Lorenzo shrugs, "We're in no hurry. We want to do it right. Those old people really knew what they were doing."

Archie nods. "The people that built it are buried right under our feet. When we're finished, it will be sacred ground again."

Lorenzo hands down the brush and bucket. He and Archie move the scaffolding carefully. Reynaldo walks by, gives me a half smile. Something that has been holding very still inside me begins to dance.

"How's it going?" he says.

"Fine."

"Good." He disappears into his mother's house. Maybe next time we'll work together.

I'm not a romantic. When I fantasize about Reynaldo it's not about sex. I imagine us reading Antonio Machado's poetry to each other, dancing together by candlelight in the living room, walking in the hills. Concocting late-night strategies, storming the Forest Service office, lying side by side across the cattle guard on opening day at the Ski Valley. What a team!

Our Lady of the Sorrows

The Owl

One of my poetry students from Boulder called to say hello. She asked if I'm "living the life of a writer." What does that mean? I'm writing almost every day. I'm also doing laundry, taking care of the pets, biking to the post office. I'm not sure what "the life of a writer" is supposed to look like on the left bank of the Rio Hondo.

The weird thing is, nothing has really changed. Here I am again, going broke while writing, kidding myself that I'm going to sell short stories to magazines. I'm even taking another look at the erotica market. It pays well. I feel as if I'm right back where I started in Taos in 1969 when I lived in the tool shed next door to John Nichols, going broke while revising my Woodstock novel *On the Bus*, thinking that was going to launch me.

I paid most of the bills this morning. My money is going fast—only three hundred left. I paid out sixty-three dollars to the vet to get the animals their shots. Snuggles is running a low fever and is down to seven pounds. I don't want to lose her.

I've definitely hit a low point here. I'm wandering around like a golem in the middle of the night, upset about the cat and feeling very much alone. The vet wasn't sure what was wrong with Snuggles—it could be the plague or rabbit fever. If she gets really sick she would need shots twice a day at five dollars a shot. I felt dismayed. Deer mice or other rodents can carry plague—they've had one case in town and three cases of rabbit fever this week. I could get it, too. I have no idea what to do about the threat of plague. I can't keep the cat from hunting. When I got home from the vet and let her out of the car, she ran off. I sat down on the step and wept.

Later I fixed myself a nice dinner, baked three little brown trout stuffed with dried mint and brushed with melted butter. With rice and salad it was perfect. After dinner I went straight to bed—too early, I guess. I woke up again at 12:30. Drank a cup of chamomile tea and went out on the trampoline.

I lay looking up at the shattered stars thinking this is part of breaking up, living alone, making the transition. It's not going to be all ecstatic dancing in the living room. When I begin to feel rushed and pressed for time because summer is running out, I have to remind myself how lucky I have been to have this time to live alone without any demands. I know that if I take even a part time job it will carry me off in another direction. I have been wondering if I should apply for the job with the recycling center. Am I a fool to pin all my hopes on writing again?

I dragged out one of my novels last week and got to work. It's like Annie Dillard's metaphoric lion—I've neglected it for so long, it's going to take a chair and a whip to tame it. I should stick to it until I've exhausted all the possibilities and I'm forced into a different channel or until I've kicked open the door to the publishing world. In my heart I believe I'm going to sell this book. Or the next one. Or the one after that. I have a trunk full of unpublished manuscripts now. The thing about writing out of your own life is that it takes time—time to live it.

I ran into John Nichols sitting outside at Dori's coffee shop where he used to write every morning. He and Aaron used to play tennis and John and I were neighbors when we both lived on Ranchitos Road. We've watched each other wallow through so many transitions over the years. When Aaron and I decided to make it legal, John asked if he could come to our wedding. His former girlfriend Stephanie was my best woman. The wedding was a simple affair in the judge's home. I remember sheep on the lawn and two-year-old Rachel turning somersaults in her blue velvet dress. Afterward we went back to John's house and finished off a bottle of wine.

At Dori's, John and I sat outside at the picnic table. He seemed to be in pretty good shape, considering that he had a heart condition and had just broken up with his second wife, the redheaded fireball, Juanita. I recall her version of her first visit to John in Taos. She drove into town and called him from a gas station. He said, "Where are you?" She said, "At the gas station across from the hospital." He said, "There is no gas station across from the hospital." She said, "Oh yes there is. I'm standing here." She climbed back into her car thinking, "Oh boy, this is going to be trouble."

I remember their wedding reception—how they laughed and fed each other cake from the end of a long, sharp knife. "I had a hunch that wasn't going to work," I said.

"Oh hell, it was a lot of fun. Wouldn't have missed it. But, Phaedra, she got the house."

"Oh, John, it's your own fault."

Unfair. I had only heard her version of it.

He leaned both elbows on the table and clasped his hands. "I had a lot of ties to that piece of land. I planted trees there, worked on the ditch." He leaned back and let his arms dangle. "But there's a time to let go of that, too. I bought a worthless piece of land way the hell out on the other side of the Gorge that nobody would want."

I was hard on him the way you are sometimes with old friends. "Are you just going to keep getting married again and again?"

He gave me a look. "No. I'm going to die."

"Me too. But it's okay. I wouldn't want to do this forever."

He laughed and agreed.

We ordered breakfast. While we were waiting I picked up my guitar and played a tune I had written about my break-up with Aaron, "The Walking Talking Blues."

"Nice," he said. He took the guitar and played his break-up song, slapping the wood, belting out his pain. He handed the guitar back and gave me a boyish grin. "Not quite as gentle as yours."

He asked if I was "working." I told him I had dragged out an unfinished novel and was wrestling with it. He told me he writes a book a year and many of them are still unpublished. He's so positive about life—both the ups and downs—he always makes me feel better.

Saturday morning I got up early to irrigate. The water in the Atalaya is so low I couldn't divert it into the pipe without blocking the ditch with a board. My main feeder ditch through the orchard is choked with willows. I've got to get out there with the clippers. I discovered that by digging just ahead of the trickle of water I can scrape out each channel a few inches deeper. At this rate, it will take all summer. Nevertheless, by blocking this channel and opening that one, I managed to get water to the thirsty trees. It took hours.

I was out there in the middle of the day in a denim skirt without hat or gloves. My cheeks were burning, sweat trickled down my face, my hair stuck to my forehead, and a blister broke on my palm. My tennis shoes were soaked, my legs splattered with mud. I cast off my skirt and dug in my underpants. "I must look like a crazy woman," I muttered. "Why am I doing this?"

I leaned on the shovel and watched the muddy trickle push through the dry brush toward the fruit trees. "I'm doing it for you," I told them. "Because you're alive."

Only the trees close to the ditch decided to bloom this year, but I should have enough fruit this fall to can some and give some to Eloy. I came back to the house to shower. In the mirror my face was as red as a radish. Next time, sunblock and gloves.

In the afternoon I did what I swore I wouldn't—dressed up in lipstick and earrings and dropped by Reynaldo's mother's house to give them some homemade cupcakes. Reynaldo answered the door.

"Hi, Reynaldo."

He frowned. "Ray. After all, it's the nineties."

I made a face. The hard English syllable drained the romance out of his name. "I'll try to get used to it."

I told him how I ran into Henry Miera, former president of the Committee To Save The Rio Hondo who said we should have a meeting to elect new officers. "What about the paperwork? I'll bet you're behind on it."

"Nothing is happening on that. We were waiting for you to get back." He smiled for the first time. I felt a stir just standing beside him. He's charming when he smiles.

———————

A meeting of the CTSRH, not the "committee" anymore, but "the community," Ted Green says. I was early and wandered around the playground. So many memories. Aaron put a lot of energy into this school. As president of the PTO he wrote a grant for the playground equipment. We installed the swings and slide and paved the playground. With the help of Connie and a couple of other parents, we got down on our knees and painted the lines on the basketball court.

Always willing to make a fool of himself for the children, Aaron played Santa at school just before Christmas and I helped him set up the spook house for Halloween. I spent many hours as teacher's aide, but in the end all the other Anglo parents in the valley car-pooled their kids to private schools in Taos. Ours were the only blondies left. They were shunned and picked on. Brian and Rachel had no friends to say good-bye to when we moved into town.

Out of the dusk a man came striding up—Ted with his energetic daughter bouncing a basketball and his sturdy son keeping pace with him on a bicycle. He gave me a nod. Then came Henry, tall and lean, president of the Committee for the past three years and eager to resign.

When we were all seated at the cafeteria tables, we had twelve people, all the regular players except Connie. I heard she had taken a job in Santa Fe and came home on the weekends. Trina was the only other female in the room, a middle-aged woman who runs a bed and breakfast in her home at the other end of the valley. Ray looked happy to be there. I was pretty lit myself.

I had forgotten how the committee works—not by parliamentary procedure, for sure—but no one person seemed to dominate. Anyone who wanted to talk just jumped in. We made motions and left them lying while we wandered through a maze of related issues. People tried to explain the history of the committee to a newcomer who said he was a friend of the guy who runs the sewage treatment plant up at Taos Ski Valley. He said the plant operators didn't see eye-to-eye with the Ski Valley at all.

I was nominated for "interim" president and everyone else agreed to serve as "interim board members" until we could get revved up again. I offered to do a newsletter and Reynaldo said he might help with that. We got up a working committee to think about a booth for Fiesta at *Nuestra Señora de los Dolores.* Ray and his brother and a handful of others have revived the traditional annual fiesta in Hondo in order to raise money for the reconstruction of the church. They have never made much more than two thousand dollars, but Archie said every penny of it goes for materials. All the labor has been volunteer. They invite all the famous dance groups in the area and favorite bands. Ortiz tells them, "All we can pay you is our prayers and our food." Thirty or forty people from the village are plastering on Saturday. Ray didn't tell me.

When it was over Ray disappeared out the door. I was trying to juggle all the stuff I'd brought. Ted offered to carry my box to the car. Wish it had been Ray. He has never shown a spark of interest in me. I've made all the moves. I've got to stop. I was getting all worked up looking at his beautiful, brown skin.

I came home feeling excited about working on the newsletter with Ray and Ted. I was tempted to ask Ray over early Thursday night to eat with me, but I didn't. I'm not going to pursue him. I shouldn't. All this very firmly to myself after waking up from an erotic dream about him.

Thursday evening—I got dressed up—big mistake. Put on my best earrings, bought chips and beer. Nobody showed for a long time. Ted had called to say he'd be about ten minutes late. I was sitting at the outside table watching the light change across the fields, playing my guitar, feeling sorry for myself.

At dusk Reynaldo sauntered around the corner of the house. I was so annoyed that everyone was late that I kept playing. He stood there, hands on his hips, "Are we having a meeting?"

"I hope so." I lay my guitar aside and tucked back my hair. I showed him my design for the logo for the newsletter. He had some ideas for improving it. Soon Ted arrived, fresh from his shower. I got out the chips and beer and we sat talking until late.

I gave them what I had written for the newsletter and a brief history of the Committee. They filled me in on what had gone down over the past five years. When it was too dark to see I brought out the lantern and lit it. Something skimmed my left shoulder and hit the screen. The guys gasped. I turned to see a pigmy owl clinging to the screen. It hung there, staring at me, then flew away.

I took it as a sign—to go deeper into the unconscious instead of mooning over Reynaldo's grainy smell, his brown face in the flickering light of the lantern. I wonder how much of this he's picked up on, how needy I seem.

As he was leaving—in spite of the warning voice inside—I asked very meekly if he could help me dig out some of my lateral ditches. He said he'd be over tomorrow, probably around lunchtime.

The Studio

*T*he morning is bright and I'm happy because I think Reynaldo is coming. I dress in my jeans and sleeveless green cotton shirt that shows off my tanned shoulders. My jeans fit well because I've lost weight. I'm feeling good. I sip a cup of coffee and try to get down to work.

I glance at the clock. Already past noon. I'm so nervous my stomach feels rumbly. I swig some Pepto Bismol.

An hour later, the clouds roll in. I have to shut down the computer in case of a lightning strike. I watch the rolling gray sky, the wind in dark branches, birds soaring in their element. I prop my feet up on the window sill and watch the whole thing unroll before me—lighting bolts, drenching rain, the smell of ozone.

I imagine Ray has had to stop work, that he will show up any minute, hair dripping, his shirt clinging to him. I imagine kissing him. Rumble rumble. I swig some Pepto Bismol.

Two o'clock. I'm pacing the living room, more and more pissed that he refuses to help, and doesn't call either. Mad at myself for asking. More Pepto Bismol.

I don't find out until much later that he was working outside, got drenched in the storm and went home to shower and rest.

At five-thirty I peer out the back door, "That's it. I'm done." So it's over before it began. Thank you, owl. My only consolation for playing the fool is that it provides comic relief. Ray, if you're reading this, I hope you're laughing, too.

The Vecinos

*T*he air is like spun honey. The roadside is crowded with the cheerful yellow faces of sunflowers. Purple asters bloom across the field and the orange mallow is a couple of feet high. Driving to town across the top of the mesa, I enjoy a wide view of tawny meadows all the way to Taos and across the Gorge to the dark rim of mountains. Beneath enormous skies a fleet of lazy clouds, outlined in charcoal, are sailing on the horizon like ships with rolling prows that taper toward the sterns.

At dusk, feeling lonely, I walked down the hill and across the wooden bridge to the big house next door to pay a visit to the *vecinos*, the neighbors. On the front porch a hammock still hung in the shade where Yona and Rachel used to lie and read to each other on summer afternoons. The house was built by Harvey Mudd, who purchased this whole end of the valley around 1967. He was a generous man; before he moved to Santa Fe he donated to the village several acres of land in upper Hondo that were utilized for a fire station, a basketball court and a baseball field. He and Aaron were best friends from their days at a private school in California. Harvey lived in our old adobe while he was building the big house. When he started pouring cement for the massive walls, the villagers thought he was damming the Rio Hondo.

Only strangers used the front door. I walked through the garage and tapped on the glass of the kitchen door. David sat at the dining room table reading a magazine, turning the pages with long, slender fingers. "Come in."

I nodded hello. "Is Ellen around?"

He waved toward the barn. I sat down and gazed out at their superb view of the mountains. Ellen crossed the upper pasture with an armful of hay and tossed it over the fence to the stallion.

David and I chatted in a very neutral way, but he perked up when I asked him what he'd been doing for exercise. "Not enough."

He told me about a trail ride he and Ellen had taken recently, camping out near Black Lake. He rode his favorite horse, Shalako, and had tied her right next to the tent. "I fell asleep in the aspen meadow with my hat over my face. Shalako nodded out just above me." He grinned. "Someone took a picture of that."

"I'd love to have that kind of trust with a horse," I said. "Do you remember the one that died in the driveway?"

"No. I think that was before my time."

In the late sixties and early seventies, Taos was crawling with hippies who found shelter in tents and buses, on communes and in the hills all around: Five Star, New Buffalo, the Hog Farm, and just up the hill from us, Morningstar and Reality Construction Company.

Inspired by a deep sense of connection at the Woodstock music festival, organizers came to New Mexico afterward looking to buy land for Earth People's Park where the "tribe" from Woodstock could re-create a communal life.

The locals called it, "the hippie invasion" and they came to the early planning meetings to say loud and clear, "There isn't enough water."

Many of the hippies were city folk, Up-Against-the-Wall Motherfuckers and other desperadoes. But New Buffalo had strong leaders, gardens, goats, construction crews with ideals and adobe bricks. Others such as the Hog Farm where I lived for a month or two, had greasy dishwater and chaos. Up at Morningstar they had guns, drugs and anarchy, and no idea how to farm or feed themselves in the land of *poco tiempo*. But they could hunt. In the winter of 1971 they poached a whole herd of deer out of the hills.

I launched into the horse story. "A couple of days before Thanksgiving Aaron came home and said a horse was down in the driveway, its ribs showing, starving to death. She had wandered down from Reality Construction Company. Aaron noticed an empty carton of chocolate milk beside the road and a flake of hay at the mare's nose. He yanked her tail and tried to get her up, but she wouldn't budge. He got his revolver, went back and shot her."

David gave a startled grunt. I went on, "The next morning when we drove out we noticed that the hippies had butchered the mare, left the legs and taken the body. They set her head up in a snow bank to scare people driving by. Later we heard that they had eaten her for Thanksgiving."

David gestured toward the garage. "They used to come down here to steal the dog food or use the phone. Once in awhile someone needed a doctor or a ride to the hospital. I was the only one around making teepee calls."

"True. A guy showed up at our door one evening with his hand wrapped in a bloody rag—Bert somebody. Bert said he was cleaning his rifle with a comb and it went off. He had shot off a couple of fingers. Aaron drove him to the hospital and then took him back up to Morningstar. A bunch of guys were squatting around a fire making tortillas with filthy hands. Bert hunkered down and took out his pain meds. The others said, 'Hey Bert, pass those around.' And he did!"

David grinned. "I had a phone call from the Preacher the other day. Remember him?"

"Sure. What did he want?"

"He said, 'This is the Preacher. I lived in a cave up in the canyon.' I said, 'Sure, Preacher. Where are you?' 'Cincinnati.' 'Well, how are you?' He said he had a dream—he had to call and warn someone that there was buggering going on at Morningstar."

I let out a giggle. "Maybe there is."

"What about the time your brothers from the Hog Farm robbed Harvey's house?"

"Oh, that. After I left the Hog Farm and moved into town, my 'brothers' came knocking on my door asking to use the shower. Later they tracked me to Harvey's where I was house sitting. While they were here they must have checked out Harvey's collection of Indian artifacts. He had Navajo rugs and pots from San Ildefonso, silver and turquoise necklaces, Eskimo walrus tusk carvings, baskets and masks." I peered into the living room. "Actually, it was kind of spooky to be alone with all those spirits at night."

"I'll bet."

Months later when Aaron and I were out for a walk, we noticed a red VW Bug tearing out of the driveway from Harvey's, honking and whooping, with arms waving out the windows. On the roof, a lone figure stood shading his eyes, looking around.

"Go back to the house," Aaron said. "I'll find out what's going on."

The man on the roof had disappeared. When Aaron searched the upstairs he found Gus crouched behind Harvey's bed, brandishing a knife, but too drunk to use it.

"He was a little guy," Aaron said. "I figured I could take him. I hauled him out and asked him to leave. But he refused. He said he was hungry, so I opened a can of stew and heated it up for him."

Gus ate the stew, but still refused to go. Aaron picked up the phone. "I'm going to call the police. You'd better be out of here by the time they arrive."

Half an hour later when the squad car pulled up in the driveway, Gus was still sprawled in a chair at the head of the table. They shoved him up against the wall and searched him. Turquoise and silver jewelry spilled out of his pockets. The cop turned to Aaron. "This place has been robbed."

"Oh, my God!" Aaron said.

Later that day, with Harvey in tow, the police stopped the red Bug on the highway to Peñasco. The cops searched the car, but the hippies refused to open the trunk. While one cop car held them, the other drove back to Taos for a search warrant. This gave Harvey time to negotiate; he promised to drop the charges if they would return everything they had taken.

They drove up to the Hog Farm. Harvey laid a blanket on the ground and pulled out his list. The hippies went inside, brought out everything they had and he checked the items off one by one.

Harvey dropped the charges, but Gus was on probation, so he was in deep doo. A few days later a busload of hippies pulled up in our driveway and filled the living room with their unwashed bodies and the smell of patchouli. For three hours they growled and snarled at Aaron and me because Gus was still in jail. They wanted us to drop the charges against him, too, but, as Aaron explained, he was being held because he was on probation. "It has nothing to do with us. You shouldn't have left him behind."

"They were probably all stoned," David said.

"And drunk. So that was the end of my romance with the counter-culture."

David whistled through his teeth. "Luckily, we don't have anything to steal."

"Sure you do," I said. "The bath tub."

Ellen wiped her feet at the garage door and shook some flecks of hay off her T-shirt. She was looking fit, her freckled face rosy with exertion. "Well, neighbor, we haven't seen you in awhile." She gave me a hug. "Sit down. Want a glass of apple juice?"

She told me Yona was in France with her boyfriend. "They met in January when he was over here trying to photograph the Indians," she said. "Gillian is off to Guatemala."

The girls have certainly become world travelers. Looking around at the shining hardwood floors, warm spacious rooms, the kitchen bright with copper pots and pans, I felt a twang of envy. Not that I want this big house, these things, but I've always wanted a horse.

Ellen asked if I was getting a lot of writing done. I told her the plot of my novel. She admitted she would be jealous if I made a million on a book and had kudos after my name. "I don't have the self-discipline," she said. "I'd rather enjoy life and daydream about success."

David said he and Ellen are negotiating a trade on the strip of land that borders our property on the west for a piece of land in San Cristobal where they'd like to retire. "We'll keep the bottom acres by the river."

My heart was in my throat wondering if this will make it better or worse for me. I went home feeling depressed.

I have to remind myself what I'm doing here and not envy my neighbors' lifestyle. The Cohns work hard for what they have. David is an internist and Ellen is a therapist. Six days a week, I see them drive out at seven-thirty in the morning and don't see the lights of their cars gliding up the driveway until after dark.

I tell myself how lucky I am to be at home day after day. I still believe in the invisible forces, because if I don't, I really am lost. I guess that's what I'm feeling—a little lost, as if I have no identity or a purpose without community.

Autumn

Summer is closing like a huge, jeweled door. Every day the sky is pellucid blue. In the gently dying autumn the pulse of the earth slows and the valley lapses into a daydream of perfect beauty.

Pickup trucks wind down the rutted mountain roads, springs creaking under the weight of neatly-stacked pine and piñon logs, chain saws piled on top. Shepherds on foot and horseback, with shaggy black dogs darting here and there, drive their woolly masses down from the high country to graze in the valley. Back lit by the sun, each tan body is outlined by a line of light, creating a woolly pattern across the meadow.

I don't think I've ever seen a fall where the colors were so vivid, everything culminating at once, the whole valley saturated with a coppery hue. The heart-shaped leaves of the lilac bush have turned yellow, pale green and maroon. Dandelion leaves are like spilled wine; the wild plum bushes down by the Rio Hondo are waxy red, and the cottonwood leaves scatter across the meadow like amber flames. The orchard is bright with red apples, purple asters and egg-yellow chamisa. This afternoon piercing sunlight burst from beneath heavy clouds, spreading glory across the fields.

© JSPedersen

Today I was walking up the driveway, the Cohns' dogs ranging out in front of me. A few feet above us, hidden by the willows, a distinct sound prickled my ears—a large animal breathing. I froze. The dogs scrambled up into the ditch, splashed back and forth, and wandered down again.

Trembling with excitement, I climbed the bank, peered up and down the waterway and saw nothing. I crossed on the pipe and scrambled up to the wagon road. From there I'd be able to spot any motion in the willows.

I peeped over the edge of a boulder and saw just below me a brown shape lolling in the branches of the old piñon tree. From her perch, the bear had a broad view of this whole end of the valley. Her fur was thick and shiny and she looked too heavy for the branch. She stretched, her ears twitched. The dogs ran off across the bridge and home. I backed away and climbed down the hill.

Eloy dropped by. We sat at the outside table drinking cherry-lemon juice while I peeled apples and waited for the first yellow jackets to come buzzing around. He cleared his throat and rubbed his nose. "I've been talking to some people in the community who are concerned about the Rio Hondo," he began in a solemn tone. "They think a Hispano should be president of the Committee because this is a Spanish community."

I could see that. I asked if he'd do it. He said he'd think about it. He talked about a quarrel he had had with Ted Green. I said I had heard about a lot of quarrels between people in the valley. "We need to pull together or we're just throwing away our power."

He nodded and took a long sip of his juice.

I brushed away a bee. "When are you going hunting?"

"Soon. Would you like to go bow hunting with me?"

Maybe I could get a hunting story out of it. "Sure. Where do you go?"

"I have a special place that nobody knows about. It's really beautiful. I'd like to show it to you."

"Do you pray to the spirit of the elk before you shoot it?"

"In the morning before I go up the mountain I pray to God for a good hunt. I'm sure He hears me."

"She," I said showing him the fat little clay goddess I wore around my neck.

He fingered it with open curiosity. "Whatever. God as Earth. To me, God is honoring my parents first of all and taking good care of them, then sharing and helping other people."

I told him the story of Siddhartha and how he reached enlightenment. He listened patiently. I showed him a picture of the Buddha and he recognized the image.

"I thank God for everything every day," he said. "And for those apples in your orchard that the birds are about to gobble up. Let's pick them together."

We made an apple-picking date for Friday afternoon.

I copied and distributed around town a hundred newsletters for the CTSRH. I never received Ray's drawing for the logo. When I dropped by to pick it up, he was on the phone. He gave me such a frown and kept me waiting for so long that I left.

Eloy came by in the late afternoon. We drove down to the orchard and picked apples standing in the back of his truck. They're big and rosy, store-sized, with the juicy tang of autumn. We laughed and talked as we filled the barrels.

He asked me what time I get up, what I eat, what I do all day. I was flattered by his curiosity. His life is very busy. His brother is tanning an elk hide. "He stretches and salts it, scrapes off the tissue and tans it by scrubbing it with the brains."

"That's why I'm a vegetarian," I said as I climbed up into the tree to snatch the apples from the highest branches.

He grinned up at me, "You're like a *muchacha*—a teenage girl. You dance, climb trees, do all these things."

I tossed him an apple.

"Thanks," he said, catching it. "I'll accept an apple from a beautiful woman."

"I'll bet I'm not the first woman to offer a man an apple."

"¡Verdad! This is a good harvest."

He recalled a dream that was more like a memory of being out on a high plain, maybe in Spain, with wagons that carried water, going around harvesting crops. "My father was saying, 'We have to hurry and get this wheat in because it's going to be a hard winter.' I asked why we had no milk. We were eating the cow. Then we ate the horses. Then we began to die, too."

When we had filled both barrels Eloy said, "Let's sit down here in the cool of the evening under this tree."

I collapsed in a grassy place beside him. As I bit through the firm skin of my apple, tart-sweet juice sprang into my mouth. The flesh was white and cool.

We were silent, listening to the stream. "Isn't this nice?" he said, "Sitting on your own land after a hard day's work, eating the apples that you grew on your own tree? The simple things in life are the best."

I smiled. "Naturally."

I have been escaping into the aspens as much as possible— two trips to Hopewell Lake, a fifty mile drive. One of those trips was with my friend Juli, a tall, golden-haired woman.

Today she wore jeans and a flannel shirt.

We followed an elk trail along the hillside down through a cascade of aspen groves, enjoying each vista as it unfolded. Grassy paths were stippled with yellow leaves—all the gold in the world for free—happiness scattered by every gust of wind, more poignant for the falling and fading.

I turned in slow circles to absorb light and shadow, to note how the slender white trunks led my eye upward to a great shout of cumulus cloud against the blue sky. We climbed up into an aspen tree and sat on a low-hanging branch making woman-talk. Juli sang in her pure soprano: "So never leave me lonely/tell me you'll love me only . . ."

If I had been alone and leery of hunters I would have moved in silence, stayed hidden in the woods. I led Juli to a buttery-yellow grove on the edge of the meadow. She slid down with her back against a tree, pulled out her pad and wrote while I flopped back with a groan of pleasure to absorb undiluted primary colors, yellow and blue, and the mirror-like shimmer of leaves as they danced in the wind. I stroked the aspen bark, smooth as a baby's skin. The blackened branches of the dead ones rose toward the sky like antlers.

Aspens are one of the largest biological organisms in the world. Left over from the Pliocene epoch, they are no longer able to reproduce sexually. Clones spring up from the parent root. An aspen grove may comprise more than forty acres of interconnected trees. Woodcutters prefer piñon, or red pine, but aspen burns hot and doesn't leave much soot in your chimney.

Aspens that have been carved on by sheepherders, called "talking trees," are now valued for their historic significance. Shepherds used to graze thousands of sheep in these mountains. By 1910 mountain-grazing lands had been taken over by the national forest. Concerned about overgrazing, the Forest Service kept limiting permits and shortening the grazing season. Today only one large herd of sheep is still grazing in the Carson National Forest.

Larry Mondragón, now a middle-aged man, remembers his life in the mountains herding sheep at the tough and tender age of fourteen. He did it for his family, without pay, he said. It was a solitary life and one that required courage, competence and good judgment. You had to be able to handle not only thousands of sheep, but packhorses and a gun. Larry rode into the mountains on a gray mare with his six-shooter strapped to his knee. Though he was lonely, he loved it up there and felt a deep connection with the land. "It's the best life I've ever seen," he said.

Nine other members of his family also herded sheep in and around the Taos area. One of them was his grandfather, Rosalio Mondragón. His father, uncles and brothers each took a turn herding fifty or sixty thousand head of sheep in the Sangre de Cristo Mountains. In May the Mondragóns drove their flocks from Llano Quemado to the top of U.S. Hill south of Taos where they ranged through the high country until snow forced them down in early September.

Sheepherders would set up camp—tents or teepees—close to a spring near the top of the mountain. They were able to scare off bears and mountain lions, but found themselves at the mercy of violent summer storms. In the dark of night, in screeching wind and drenching rain, a powerful bolt of lightning struck Rosalio's teepee. He was burned and knocked unconscious. He woke some time later with a dislocated shoulder, in pain, but glad to be alive. Hiking down the trail the next day, he fell and knocked his shoulder back into place.

To while away the time, sheepherders often carved on the aspens—nothing deep enough to kill the trees. A light touch of a penknife was enough to peel away the bark and leave a mark. Some had their own signature such as an elk head. One untutored youngster progressed from block print to a curving line as he taught himself to write.

Maria García documented a broad range of carvings from religious to humorous: crosses, hearts pierced by Cupid's arrow, naked ladies, horses carved in a ring around the tree, dogs, cattle, phonetically written messages, and once, a whole poem. One abashed sheepherder was given his pink slip in the tree bark and told to go home without pay because he lost the entire flock.

The sun was about to slide behind the mountain, and lavender shadows claimed our grove. Juli shivered and stood up. "We'd better find the car. It's going to get cold."

As we climbed out of the valley we joked about getting lost.

"They found her a week later, naked and frostbitten," I said.

"She wouldn't talk about it—said she didn't remember what happened."

I spotted the shine of a vehicle through the trees. "Let's sneak up on them."

"Why?"

"Because I'd rather sneak up on them than have them sneak up on us."

We peered out from behind a tree and giggled. The vehicle was mine.

On the way home I told Juli my "hiding" story. Rachel was nine, moping around the house on a beautiful autumn day. I invited her to take a drive with me up into the aspens. We traveled four miles up a bumpy back road into a canyon. I parked behind a small hill in a hollow.

Rachel was examining the puzzle pieces of bark on a ponderosa pine, enjoying the vanilla scent, when a battered pickup pulled into the clearing. Four blue-jeaned men hopped out and grabbed their rifles. A couple of them were glugging Budweisers.

I whispered to Rachel, "Let's get out of here. Think yourself invisible. Keep this big tree between us and them. Walk in a straight line over the hill and don't look back."

We retreated over the hill and paused beside a pit. The massive roots of a ponderosa had torn a crater in the earth when the tree fell. "Let's rest here for a minute," Rachel said.

Her instincts were right on. As we sat down, a shot exploded. I grabbed Rachel and hit the ground. We lay clutching each other as more shots rang out. No way to tell if the men were headed toward us—better try to get to the car. As bullets whistled over our heads we crawled on our bellies just below the ridge, then dropped into the hollow where our car was parked.

We scrambled into the Subaru and locked the doors. I let out a sigh of relief and reached in my pocket. My keys were gone.

"Shit!" Nothing to do but go back for them. "After I leave, lock my door," I told Rachel. "If I'm not back in ten minutes wait until it's quiet. Then walk out to the road and get help. Don't let anyone see you until you get to the highway."

With Rachel secure, my fear fell away. I crawled back along the way we had come, following a trail of Juicy Fruit gum that had fallen from my shirt pocket. Now and again a random shot went off.

When I reached the crater I found the keys—I had dropped them when the first shot banged. It didn't take long to crawl back to the car. Rachel was sitting in the front seat, her face red and streaked with tears. "I thought you were going to get killed."

She sobbed on my shoulder while I held her. When the blast of guns stopped and I heard the truck leave, I started up the engine and drove out of there.

——— ——— ———

Aaron frowned and scoffed when he heard the story. "They didn't know you were there. Why didn't you shout and tell them to stop?"

"With Rachel there, I wasn't willing to risk it."

"You're paranoid. They wouldn't have hurt you."

"They were drinking."

"Lots of men have a beer or two when they go hunting. I used to hunt with my dad. They were all decent men. Hunters don't turn into monsters when they go out in the woods."

Juli shook her head. "When I'm out in the woods alone I hide, too."

Back at her house, I told my story to her husband. Martin said, "I don't want to run into anybody when I'm out there alone. I might slip behind a boulder or a tree to avoid an encounter."

You, too, eh?" I smiled at the image of hunters marching off into the wilderness while up and down the trail cautious hikers peered at them from behind boulders and trees.

Elk Hunt

*T*he western sky is a delicious peach color, deepening to magenta, as we rumble up the dirt switchbacks heading for base camp in Eloy's battered Ford pickup. He slows for the humps that have been bulldozed to control run-off, while I clutch the dashboard and peer over the drop-off. Through the mist of the valley below, the lights of Questa twinkle amber and pale green.

A full moon rises above the tops of the pines as we arrive at his camp and unload our gear. Eloy is packing a seventy-five pound bow, a Brownie Drake Flight Master. He tests the string. "It takes a lot of strength to pull a bow like this, especially when you're sitting down."

In his leather sheath he carries five arrows with 125 Tri-Max three-faced blades. He slides one out to show me and touches the tip with a callused thumb. "They cut good," he says. "They're inexpensive and they work great."

He has already set up a Hillary tent that has seen him through some wilderness adventures. Scrawled over the door in mud are the words, "We don't die, suckers!"

There's plenty of room inside. We unroll our sleeping bags and crawl into them. As the night wind wafts through the pines, he tells me about the legend on the tent face. "It seems like every three years we get snowed in on the October rifle hunts. This is the only tent that's survived. The rest got broken."

He rolls up on one elbow to face me. All I can see is the silhouette of his large, shaggy head. He smells of leather and leaves. "I was hunting with my four brothers in late October in the San Juans. We set the base camp five miles inside the Cruces Basin. That whole night it thundered and poured. Then the rain turned to snow. About ten the tent poles broke under the weight. That was the most miserable night of my life," he says without rancor. "We had to tear a hole in the tent to get air. The snow fell in and melted on us. The next morning we got up at dawn. We had to cut through the canvas to get out. We saddled up our horses. We had about two feet of snow and it was still coming down. We rode around in circles the whole day and finally got back to our base camp around four in the afternoon. By then we had three and a half feet of snow. We ended up sleeping in the truck for three nights until the snow melted enough to get out."

"Jeez. . . . So it ruined your hunt. Too bad."

He snorted. "We still got our elks—on snowshoes. We brought out four elks on that trip."

I wake an hour before dawn and lie quietly with my eyes closed until Eloy touches my arm. "It's time to get up."

We dress in camouflage, eat a couple of apples and bananas and Eloy zips up the tent. He walks out into the meadow and stands quietly, his hair blue-black in the morning sun, cheeks pink, dark eyes raised to a flawless sky. "Please Lord, bless this hunt that we're going on, and bless my friend Phaedra. Thank you God for the elk, for the beautiful mountain, for my beautiful friend and this beautiful day."

He drapes his bugle around his neck, dons his sheath of arrows, picks up his bow and we are off up the steep hillside through the woods, careful not to crack any branches. I'm in hiking boots, but he's surefooted in Reeboks.

118

I'm panting as we reach the top of the ridge. We stand looking west at mountainside warm with morning sun. This part of the forest has been burned to a crisp. Nothing is left to interfere with our view but dead aspen trees. Eloy picks up a piece of charred wood, rubs it on his hands and blackens my face. He pushes back a strand of hair on my forehead. "You look cute."

I take the burned stick and blackened his face, even his ears, while my genes reverberate with ancient memory—primal invocation. "I go nature's way," Eloy says. "Some hunters buy stuff to blacken their faces, but I like to use soot. They smear themselves with rotten stuff to knock out the human scent, but you don't have to do that. I like to wear clean clothes. I don't cook anything with outdoor fires or touch any gasoline."

He hoists his bow. "Let's go. Try to walk in tandem with me like we're the same animal."

I follow in his footsteps through a dream-like forest, blackened skeletons of pines and bone-white aspens innocent of bark, silky as soap. Beneath our feet are asters and large, vibrant rose hips. My hands are freezing. I should have worn gloves. My nose is running like a leaky faucet—from the soot?

Eloy pauses near a bedraggled pine. "This is a shed," he whispers. "This is where the elk come to rub their antlers, mark their territory and work off their frustrations." He holds up one finger. "Do you hear that?"

We fall silent, ears cocked. The rasping note of a bull elk, like a strangled bagpipe, floats up from the pine forest below. We sit down on a log. Eloy lifts his horn and bugles the male call a few times. No answer.

"I rifle hunt in Colorado, too," he says, "but I love the thrill of hunting with a bow, hearing them bugle, bugling back, playing with the elks. I like the challenge. I respect the elk for what it is. I've shot thirteen elks with a bow, one every year since I started hunting."

We creep through lush timothy grass, up to our thighs. Here

the new aspens are already three feet high. Far below us, several elk bugle back and forth in the still morning air.

"When the elks bugle at the first stages of the rut, they're trying to attract the two-year-old cows," Eloy whispers. "They can have a herd of up to three hundred cows. The bulls are challenging each other. The cows are answering back to the bulls. Elks are very vocal. That's what makes them different from hunting deer."

Eloy tucks in his chin and conjures up a female call from deep in his throat.

"Where did you learn how to do that?"

"I learned it over the years. You can't help but get better at what you do. It's good to be able to do both kinds of calls. Sometimes you lose your bugle. And sometimes you lose your voice."

I sense movement. Suddenly, to our left at the top of the rise, a mature elk appears outlined against the sky, antlers lifted high.

We sit still as stumps. Eloy tucks in his chin and bugles the female call. Pauses. Calls again. Pauses. Calls again. The elk swivels his head this way and that and drifts down the hillside toward us.

"It's too small, only a six pointer," Eloy says. "I'll call it in closer so you can take a picture." The elk wanders to within thirty feet of us. "Take the picture," Eloy urges, but trees are in the way. The bull looks straight at us without seeing us. We are like mythical characters in magic cloaks, invisible. With his bugle dangling between his knees, Eloy looks like the great god Pan in blackface.

With a slow and stately stride, the elk passes down the hill and disappears into the woods below.

"It's too bad you didn't get a picture," Eloy says.

"Sorry."

He shrugs. "That's okay."

We head back to camp for lunch. He feels sure the elk will graze their way back to the timothy grass in the afternoon and he'll get one then, but he's wrong. In the afternoon the elk quit bugling. I don't know if I'm disappointed or relieved.

I have vivid memories of a wounded doe that staggered down

from the hills and collapsed in front of the studio, long graceful legs buckling. I crept close and gazed into the dark round eye, glazed with pain. Her head slumped to the ground; her back leg was mangled, bleeding from a bullet hole. She had come down to the river to die.

Aaron, who never allowed anyone to cross the property with a gun, went back to the house for his rifle. He's not a hunter, and I gave it up forty years ago when I left Michigan, but a gun comes in handy once in awhile.

I turned my face away as he took aim. The blast of his 30.06 rang across the meadow and washed against the rocky mouth of the canyon, violence swallowed by the silence, like a held breath.

I murmured a prayer of thanks for her life, squatted beside her and slit open her hide along the belly. I picked off a swollen tick and peeled back the skin. I sawed off the legs at the knees, cutting through sinew and glistening bone. Panting, I sliced through the muscles of the neck, severing the spine, bloody hands brushing back strands of hair that stuck to my cheek. Panting.

I divided the meat into meal-sized chunks for a family of four, sanctified them with Saran wrap and popped them in the freezer for venison stew and steak and chile. To honor the life of the wounded doe, we ate her piece by piece. We became her and she became us, but she was stringy as fear and tough as pain going down.

I flaked three bars of Ivory soap into a washtub full of water and soaked the hide for a week. It came out tanned and clean, the hair intact. I draped it over the trunk to dry; it stiffened to the rectangular shape and lay there all winter to remind me that I, too, am here to feed and nurture the land, to be consumed by it, invaded and conquered from within.

———— ———— ————

"I could have had that one," Eloy says. "That one was mine. But I usually let the first one go. Why shoot a small elk when you can have a big one? I got several elks that could easily score on the books. There's always bigger bulls. But if you can't get a big one"—his blackened face breaks in a white-toothed grin—"then take whatever comes by."

Back at camp we wash the soot off our faces with soap and water. Eloy cooks lunch—slabs of elk steak with homemade tortillas and slices of roasted green chile. He wraps the elk steaks in foil, heats them over the burner of his Coleman stove and warms the tortillas the same way. In the cool mountain air, sunlight warm on our cheeks, we devour our lunch. For dessert his mother has made an apricot pie, sweet and tangy and cold.

Eloy says, "This steak was from an elk I shot last fall."

"Tell me about it."

"It took a long time, but I called it to within thirty feet," he says. "It was walking toward me, but it didn't see me. The arrow hit it in the chest with a thunk, like a fist hitting a book. It stumbled, went off into the trees."

He looks at me. "I've learned not to run after them. About twenty minutes later I heard the air whoosh out of its lungs. I found it lying on the ground. I threw a stone at it to make sure it was gone. Then I gutted it, and cut the balls off so the taste wouldn't contaminate the meat. I quartered it, covered it with branches and went for the horses."

I can imagine him leading the brown gelding along the high mountain ridge bearing its heavy burden, quartered elk wrapped in an old tarp that wouldn't disguise the scent of blood. Pressing forward through the twilight, glancing over his shoulder, wary of mountain lions.

"Our grandpas were probably the first to hunt elk around here," he says. "We're simple people and it's very sacred to us—something we don't take for granted. In the early 1900s trappers and miners almost completely wiped them out. Thanks to the stud laws and transplanting, they've made a great comeback."

When Eloy gets home he will slide the meat in the cooler, slice up some of it for steaks and freeze them. With the rest he makes jerky. "I slice a chunk of meat, sprinkle it with salt and pepper and green chile. Others like to soak it with lemon and red chile, but I like green—it's hotter. Then I cut it in narrow strips and hang it to dry on the *vigas*. It takes about ten days for the jerky to cure well. I store it in flour sacks hanging in the cupboard, ready to eat any time."

He smiles and touches my cheek. "Even though we didn't kill an elk today, I'll see that you get some elk steak, *muchacha*. We like to share the meat with our friends and neighbors. There's gonna be enough in the freezer to last a whole year."

Giving Thanks

By November the color has drained out of the landscape, leaving it dull and sere. Not my favorite month. During the winter I miss the colors more than I mind the cold. I dry my fall leaf collection between the pages of the phone book, then pin them to my white lampshade so every time I turn on the light their ruddy colors shine through.

When I walked down to the bridge this morning I startled a great blue heron. Trailing long legs straight behind, it flapped off slowly toward the canyon on curved wings about six feet across. It's the second time I've seen it. Some of them migrate here from Utah and Nevada for the winter, and some are year-round residents. I'm often surprised by the variety of bird life that can be sustained in the high mountain desert. I've seen bald eagles diving for fish in the Rio Grande, and one April day, a small flock of migrating pelicans swimming in the middle of the river.

Aaron invited me up to Boulder for Thanksgiving—if my car could make it. I had just turned over a hundred thousand miles on the old Toyota Tercel. The weather report said freezing rain in the late afternoon. I labored up La Veta pass while the road was still dry. Coming into Denver, fog shrouded the highway. I couldn't see more than twenty-five feet ahead of me. Traffic slowed to a crawl.

The weatherman on the radio warned everybody to slow down. "It's only going to get worse." Instead of slowing down, traffic was speeding up. Shaken by fatigue and the thought of the ordeal ahead, I stepped on the gas. I wanted to make the most of the dry roads and get in before dark.

I decided to avoid the traffic around Denver and cut over to Golden. Good choice. Five minutes later the news said a truck was upside down on I-25 and traffic was backed up for miles. Ten miles out of Boulder the roads were slick with ice, and snowfall was darkening the skies behind me.

I arrived at sunset just as Aaron was about to leave to see his girlfriend Sheila off at the airport. He was looking attractive in his maroon sweater. I felt dismayed. Rachel says he dates more than she does. Well, what did I expect?

Winter. Cold. Snow down your collar. I'm sitting in Aaron's apartment overlooking Boulder Creek. Big snowflakes are twirling down into the ebony water that flows under ink-black branches trimmed with snow. Hope I can get home again.

I spent last evening with Rachel and her girlfriend Loris. Rachel is scrambling to get registered for next semester, which they do by phone, dialing and redialing until they connect with the courses they want. She looked tired, subdued, but gave me a big hug and seemed glad to see me. We went out for dinner at The Harvest, very pleasant. I called about half the people I wanted to see; they were either busy or out of town. Tomorrow I will go out and buy the turkey and trimmings. I offered to cook the dinner.

The sun rises over the snowy streets of Boulder. Skies are clear and it's very cold. I spent most of today driving in circles between Safeway and King Soopers. Rachel came with me. We kicked up our heels in the parking lot, singing an ironic tune, "We're going to the store/We're going to the store/We love the stuff, we have enough/But we want more!"

In the afternoon I baked a couple of pies—pumpkin and pecan—while Rachel sat on the counter reading "MacBeth" aloud to me.

After dinner Aaron and I had a long talk. I owe him about seven hundred dollars for my half of the taxes and insurance on the house. Instead of the money, he'd like me to build a storage shed on the property where he can store his things while he wanders the world. I asked why he wouldn't let me use the couch and table. He said he was afraid if I left and rented out the house, the tenants would trash the furniture. I said I wasn't going anywhere, but he didn't believe me.

"I've put a lot of work into fixing up and maintaining the place," I said. I wanted some recognition of that.

His eyes widened. "So now you're going to claim the house by strength of your devotion to the property?"

I pulled back. "Hey, that's an attack on my character."

"You're paranoid."

An uneasy laugh. "No, you're the one that's paranoid."

He turned to me. "What I'd really like to hear is that you're not going to try to wrest my half of the property away from me."

I looked him in the eye. "I am not going to try to wrest your half of the property away from you."

He sighed, got up and paced the room, hands in his pockets. "If it was just me, I'd sell it, but there are all these other people involved. Rachel feels very attached to the Hondo house. And it gives me an ongoing sense of family."

He sat down beside me on the couch. "That's also why I don't want to sever the connection between us. Yet."

We were both silent, searching each other's faces. I said, "I think Rachel is hoping we get back together."

He rubbed his forehead, ran his fingers through his dark

mane of hair. "It doesn't seem likely. I think the old patterns would quickly reassert themselves."

"I've changed," I said. "I'm learning to express my feelings in the moment of feeling them instead of clamming up."

"That's always been an issue for you."

I fingered the piping on the arm of the couch. "You know, I often wanted you, but I couldn't say so. I'm sorry for that."

"You always left it up to me to make the first move." He let out a short sigh. "I realize I'm a very dominating person. It's my strength, but it's also my weakness."

"Where did that come from?"

He made an impatient gesture. "Oh, my mother infused me with a false sense of my own self-importance. We don't change. We can only become who we are. I'm in conflict being in a relationship. I can't have her and still have myself. I'm probably going to end up alone in some cheap rented room. Like my mother—I have no desire to live to be really old."

I sat up straight. "I'd like to live long enough to reach my highest potential."

He snorted and laughed. "You're going up. I'm going down."

As for me, I feel sure that I'm not going to spend the rest of my days alone. But even if I do, it's okay. It has to be. The main thing is the journey itself. I'm working on gradually letting go of material things, of my addiction to the ecstatic moment, pleasure for its own sake, longing that is always frustrated by falling short of an all-embracing love. Maybe this hunger is an intrinsic part of the human condition since the first breath when we were squeezed out of the garden into the cold reality, the cord cut forever. Theologians say this sense of emptiness can only be filled by God.

"When I returned to Hondo I had to face the void inside me," I said. "Instead of trying to stuff it with a new relationship, I filled it with silence."

He nodded. "I understand that."

I smiled. "You're one of the few people who would."

He may not express it or actively seek it, but I see how he continues to grow, in his poetry, in his own letting go. We evolve through life whether we want to or not.

When we had gotten all that out, he grinned and slapped my knee. "Good talk."

A little tension there, but it was real.

I wake up on Aaron's couch resigned to my loneliness and the lack of touching. I want to go on no matter what comes next. It begins to feel like freedom. I feel centered in a new and more constant way by what I have voluntarily given up. Something else comes to fill the void and sustain me.

I can bear pain and loss; what I can't bear is being imprisoned. My heart feels as if it is opening and opening, and as it does I get lighter and lighter. The grief and tears are mingled with the joy, the anger with the love. If I love and have nothing at stake, no one can ever take my life away from me. I am prepared to be a wanderer in the world just as much as I am prepared to go home and live quietly alone.

Thanksgiving Day

Aaron has been very appreciative of me "coming in and doing a little cooking, a little cleaning, a few repairs." (Nothing really— I fixed the plant table, washed the kitchen floor, re-screwed the handle on the pot.) He thanked me for doing the shopping and cooking. "I'm exhausted. I've been terribly busy."

This time we didn't have too much conflict in the kitchen. His way of cooking is a lot different from mine, but this time I let it go. I used to want the holiday meals to be perfect, and anything less upset me.

The guests arrived around two: Aaron's younger sister, Anna, and her partner Richard and daughter Nadia, and Rachel's friend Loris. Anna was looking good in an India print blouse and a long skirt, her black hair loose over her shoulders. Her lean brown face shows her age only in the crinkles around the corners of her eyes. She and Richard, a quiet and sweet-natured young man, are working for a small company that sells natural soaps, herbs and essences. She said, "Sometimes I look around and say, `What am I doing here in Boulder?' When I think of settling down I consider going back to Taos, but sometimes I don't want to be anywhere. I feel disconnected, like—don't you want to be on this planet?"

I nodded. I've had exactly the same feelings. The spirit of place is not as important as being with the people you love. As I grow older, I think that's all that really matters. Of course, it would be nice to have both.

I slid the turkey out of the oven—done to a golden brown. Many helpers set things on the table. We sat down and held hands around the table for a moment, a ritual Aaron would just as soon skip. Anna shortened the blessing to a resonant chord that ran around the table and broke in laughter: "Yummmmmm!"

The taste of warm, succulent turkey with chilled cranberry sauce and my mother's special stuffing brought cries of delight. We dove into the pies—devoured everything in sight. Then we squeezed together on the couch and watched "Roadside Prophets."

After everyone had gone and Aaron was in bed, Rachel sat on the floor by the couch with her head on my knee, holding my hand while we talked. She told me about the various men in her life. I talked to her about the danger of merging, surrendering everything to a man, wanting to crawl inside him and take refuge.

She said she felt she was pushing herself in school and not getting the least recognition for it.

"Your dad loves you and brags about how well you're doing," I said.

She tugged on a strand of hair. "I feel like the whole reason I'm going is to please him."

I stroked her long fingers. "I'm very proud of you, too. It's so important to me that you're in school now instead of getting married like I did at your age."

She looked up at me. "And I'm really proud of you, that you've fought to face yourself and become independent."

My heart swelled like a bud in spring rain. "Every battle I win is one less you have to struggle through."

I confessed my addiction to men. "Instead of plunging into another relationship, I'm trying to build a core of self-esteem and self-sufficiency," I said. Thrusting away thoughts of Reynaldo, the owl clinging to the screen. "I hope to spend the winter writing my next book, taking care of myself."

When I suggested she build on her desire to be a counselor for adolescents she said, "I can't live to care-take others. Because the other side of that is wanting them to take care of me."

I was silent a moment, looking into her eyes. "I'm glad you see that so clearly."

She got up and put on the kettle. "I'm so sick of school I feel like leaving town."

"If you still feel that way next summer, I'll have space for you in Hondo."

She poured a cup of tea for me. "I've missed you. When I look at my friends, I realize how lucky I am to have two such great, caring parents."

"Your Dad has been working very hard to provide you with physical support."

"I know."

"His critical nature has nothing to do with who you are."

"I believe that. Now if I could just feel it."

Someday she'll get past that and be fine. But she'll have to get approval and love from the inside, not from a man.

I hung around for one more day visiting friends. In the evening Aaron and I went out to a movie. He's always early, hates crowds. He moaned as we walked through the jammed parking lot, "I should have known better than to come on a Friday night."

The movie was "Fearless" with Jeff Bridges, about the heightened reality of an air-crash survivor. We liked the scene with Bridges sitting on the ground beside his car. He spit in the dirt, rolled it into a ball, mashed it on his finger and stared at it in wonder. Then he drove with his head out the window, hair blowing.

When we came out, the wind was blowing and the night was black. Our steps rhymed as we walked to the car, arms around each other. We drove home in silence—he drove very fast shifting through the gears like a race car driver.

Back at his apartment, he fixed tea and played a tape that was part of the movie soundtrack. We sat on the couch listening to the music, eyes closed, for another half an hour, until we had both come down enough to have a normal conversation.

I love that long, shared silence. I can't imagine ever having that with anyone else. In some ways, it's more intimate than making love.

Chopping Wood

*I*t's going to be a skinny Christmas around here if I don't find work soon. I shouldn't have spent so much on presents up in Boulder, but I wanted to get that taken care of before I went broke.

Snow drifts in slanting lines from heavy skies, transforming the texture of the landscape. I had forgotten the soft beauty of winter colors, the delicacy of pale yellow grasses stiff with cold. I'd like to try to draw the scene in pastels.

After the storm I stood at the front window, looking out at the river sparkling through the trees, feeling the sun on my face, thinking how wonderful it is to be able to see flowing water from your bedroom window, when I was struck to the heart by memories of Aaron.

In the afternoon I went down to the swing. The river was high, the flat rock almost covered. I heard a shout. Ignacio Montoya and his sons were slaughtering cattle. A cow had escaped and bolted across the river to the end of the orchard. They chased it down and slaughtered it on the spot with a bullet between the eyes. They slit its throat; the blood poured out, steaming. The body trembled and convulsed. Afterward, Ocho lapped up pools of blood in the melting snow. Life is raw here, close to the surface; so is death.

Hooray! The whole family is coming home for Christmas. I took an old sleeping bag to the thrift store and traded it for a mattress for Brian. My secret hope is that he will come and spend some time with me here, living the spiritual life. I feel calm again. I am waiting like a spider in my web. Patience.

At dusk a small herd of deer drifts down from the mesa to drink from the river and graze in the field. And eat the Cohns' hay, which is stored in a shed with only a roof. David ignored these wild freeloaders for awhile, but when the bales were gutted and strewn, he tried fencing around the sides of the shed. One night a doe caught her leg in the wire. The Cohns' dogs surrounded the frantic animal, brought it down and killed it. For days fragments of bone and hide lay scattered across the yard. David took down the fence. Now when I walk past their barn I see delicate pointed deer tracks heading for the alfalfa.

Driving home from town after dark, I startled five or six deer in the driveway as I picked up the round green glow of their eyes. I slowed down. They are not like rabbits that seem to have an irresistible urge to rush across the road in front of the car.

Deer tend to pause, consider the situation for a few seconds—then flee. I tried not to rush them, but it's fun to watch them spring from powerful haunches in a slow arc over the top of the fence.

Close to the house, I saw a few more milling silhouettes on the side of the road. I braked to watch their slender legs scissoring like shadow puppets. I turned off my lights, rolled down the window and talked to them in a caressing tone. They stood still, twenty feet away, their big ears tuning me in like radar, willing to listen for as long as I was willing to talk. "You're so beautiful," I told them. "Be careful. And don't eat the Cohns' hay."

At the gas station in town I spotted an old Toyota truck, the springs sagging under a load of wood. I pulled over. Three people were squashed in the front seat: an old couple and a young man. The driver said they wanted a hundred and seventy-five for the cord. I looked it over—mostly cedar and piñon—you can't get piñon anymore. Mostly what they sell now is aspen and red pine. But some of the logs were too big for my stove. He said they'd come down to one hundred and twenty-five and chop it up for me. I glanced at the sky; thin snowflakes were drifting down. "I'll buy it."

They followed me to Hondo, backed in and unloaded the wood under my front *portal*. The young guy with a big grin and missing front teeth introduced them all around. He was Rudy and the old man with the dark, shrewd face was Manuel. The woman, Susie, had an auburn pony tail and light blue eyes. "I'm the daughter of Annie Oakley," she said.

Rudy grinned at me, "She's from England. England!"

The big logs needed to be cut with a chainsaw, but theirs had burned out on the mountain. I ran next door and borrowed one. Manuel took out his file and sharpened it. I brought the chopping log from the back of the house and Susie surprised me by sinking the ax into it. I said no, that was for chopping the smaller stuff. While Manuel had at the big ones with the chain saw, Susie took her turn chopping. "Don't get hurt, Grandma," Rudy said.

Not to be outdone, I wrapped an ace bandage around my sore arm and tried to keep up with the wood stacking. Rudy and his Grandpa made short work of it. The old guy whacked the logs in just the right spot and they fell apart. Our faces were flushed and we were all laughing.

I made tea for them. They wanted to trade another load of wood for the chainsaw, go right back up there tomorrow. "It's not going to be much of a Christmas," Susie said.

I told them sorry, the chainsaw wasn't mine, and gave them an extra twenty.

When we had finished Rudy opened his arms wide and gave

me a hug. Grandma took the money, they hopped in the truck and were gone.

I wake at dawn to a room gone cold as the tip of my nose. There's an icy spot at the bottom of the sleeping bag. I can't find my good wool socks. They're stuffed in my roller blades? I lie curled up like the dead tarantula I found on the windowsill. I picture myself getting up. Once I've done that, I've created enough momentum to struggle out of my sleeping bag and stumble to the wood box.

Great. I've forgotten to leave some kindling for morning. I've forgotten what it takes to keep up with the demands of this rural life. All I've had to do for the past ten years is nudge the wall switch up to seventy.

I pull on my jeans and scuffed cowboy boots and hurry into my down jacket. A light snow has fallen in the night; pale clouds are drifting off the massive peaks. The ax waits, poised on its tip in the chopping block where Manuel heaved it with a final authoritative swing.

I tug it out, heft it. The head of the ax is too heavy for me, the handle too long. This is a man's tool, but it takes the weight and strength of a man's ax to do this job. I will have to fit my body to the tool.

I start with something small, half a log of red pine, dry, easy to split. I swing the ax. All I have to do is hit the log, but the first blow glances off and knocks it into the snow. The next attempt slices off a three-inch chunk. Struggle. Shiver. I wrestle with the weight of the ax and fear of chopping off my toe. Get it together, Phaedra.

Look for the grain. Go with it, not against it. There's a crack in the top of the log. Try for that. But when I heave the ax above my head, the weight of the head tips me backward and throws off my aim.

How much force does it really take? Maybe not a full swing. I try it from three feet above and let the weight of the ax head carry it down. The piece splits clean. Good. Avoid the knots and branches. Don't try for the logs that are over a foot long. This chopping block is too high for you—try the lower one. Now a bigger piece, a whole log—that fat one. Keep your eye on the point where you want to strike.

I'm breathing fast, cheeks buffed by the cold, warm all over in the bracing mountain air—the wood that warms you three times, if you count stacking it. It occurs to me that wood chopping could be a meditation rather than some desperate struggle. I pretend I am a samurai warrior with a long curving sword. I place the log on the block. Pause. Center. Look up at the mountains a moment. Breathe. I stand tall with the sword—the ax—ready.

I swing like a pendulum to gain some momentum, a smooth graceful arc. Down comes the ax carried by the weight of the head with an even force behind it. I miss the center crack. Is the wood resisting? I thank the spirit of the tree for its life, for the energy that keeps us warm.

I think of Becky, a nineteen-year-old girl I picked up hitchhiking. She was tall and large-boned with a heart-shaped face and honey-colored hair that fell over her shoulders in two thick braids. Below the silky green skirt that brushed her ankles, she was wearing lace-up boots.

Her father owned a cabin near a lake in British Columbia, she told me. She decided to go up there to spend the winter alone. The cabin didn't have a double roof so the heat escaped through the ceiling. "I spent most of my daylight hours chopping wood and hauling it back to the cabin on a sled," she told me. "It was so cold that if I let the fire go out, the bucket of water beside the stove would freeze solid by morning."

I nodded. She gave me a bashful grin. "Every couple of weeks I'd go down to meet the mail boat at the end of the lake. Really, I was hoping to meet a man who was looking for a woman living alone in the woods."

But the man never showed. He was probably down in San

Francisco looking for some hippie chick with honey-colored braids. As soon as the ice broke up, she locked up the cabin and headed south.

———— ———— ————

It takes a little practice to perform the full-centered, arcing swing, to gain the confidence it takes, to know that this heavy iron head can and will split this piñon, that I will not be defeated, alone in the mountains without a man.

At last the brain stops directing. I take a deep breath. The ax, the arm and the eye all converge on the goal. Thunk! The log splits dead center right where I aimed it. I burst out laughing, pause to look up at the mountains and give thanks, to feel the strength of my body, the grace of life flowing through my lungs and heart and veins.

I sling the cut quarters across the yard toward the front door. They fall with a satisfying thud. When the stack is high enough, I give the ax one final authoritative thunk! in the center of the chopping block. I saunter into the house, arms full of logs and kindling. My coffee this morning, brewed on top of the wood stove, is the best I've ever tasted.

Winter Solstice

*T*he temperature is sinking like a lead weight, down to one degree last night. I strolled to the end of the orchard and paused beside the river, stunned by a sparkling cedar tree, crystalline snowflakes twirling down out of a clear sky, so beautiful that I cried.

In the afternoon I climbed the back hill to see if I could dig up a Christmas tree before the next storm hit, but most of them were safe beneath big rocks, frozen into the ground. A rambling search brought me to a symmetrical piñon about six feet high, just right for the corner of the living room. I said my apologies to the tree and asked it to come and be part of my Winter Solstice celebration. Then I had at it with the saw, which took about an hour, attacking from all angles, too close to the ground, trying to preserve the bottom limbs. The saw was dull and jammed in the cut, but I finally toppled the frightened tree.

Then the little matter of dragging it to the car. It was much heavier than I thought it would be. I didn't have the strength to lift it onto the roof, so I lay it across the hood and secured it with a rope between both doors. Not that I could see out my windshield. No matter. I knew where the road went. Oops! Forgot about that rock. Slow down. Peer between the branches. If anyone sees you, they'll know for a fact that you're crazy.

———— ———— ————

Two days before Christmas Aaron's Toyota pulled up in the driveway. I ran out to meet them. Aaron was sleeping in the back seat; Brian was sleeping in the front. Who was driving? Rachel! She stepped out of the car, looking tall and competent in her navy pea coat and long scarf dangling around her neck. "Hi, Mama!" She picked me up and swung me around, which always makes me squeal. The guys stretched and yawned, got out and gave me hugs.

As the sun streaked flame across the evening sky, we settled in the living room in front of the fire. They all looked cold and tired. Aaron had brought some amaretto, which we drank with ice. He also brought some new music so lovely I sank into total stillness listening to it. It was touching to see how Ocho went from one family member to the next, saying hello. Rachel sat reading to Brian in the armchair while I made burritos. Having them all here under one roof again, my heart was full.

———— ———— ————

Christmas Eve. The stockings are hung by the window with care, and Rachel helped me fill them. The presents are wrapped and the turkey is thawing in the kitchen sink. I glance out the window at the sun lying pale and distant on the horizon. We pull on extra socks, wool hats, scarves and mittens before we pile in the car. The road to the Pueblo is snow-packed. We cross the cattle guard and swing onto the back road so we can find a parking place not too far from the church.

The bonfires in front of St. Jerome chapel have already been lit. A veil of black smoke drifts into the sky. St. Jerome is a traditional example of adobe architecture with a flat roof and contoured, adobe walls. The front courtyard is surrounded by a wall about three feet high, painted at intervals with wide white stripes. We enter through a stepped arch lit by *farolitos*. Set in sand at the bottom of paper bags, the candles give off a cheerful orange glow. On each side of the heavy wooden door stands a blue spruce tree dancing with snow, draped with silver trim and a few glass balls.

Inside, the chapel is packed, glistening in silence, the pews crowded with Indians in their striped Pendleton blankets and flowered shawls. We sit at the back and I gaze around at the deep Gothic-arched windows, each one decorated with a wreath and a candle burning on the sill. The chip-carved wood pattern of the window frame complements the amber fluted glass.

Above the altar the Madonna or Corn Mother is wearing a sparkling white dress and shawl to symbolize winter. Her niche is decorated with painted cornstalks, twined with scarlet flowers. The Indians file up to the altar to touch her hem and kneel to pray. The door behind us wafts open and we catch a glimpse of flames shooting up from the bonfires inside the courtyard. In the distance—jingling ankle bells—headed our way.

An Anglo priest steps forward to relate a short simple version of the miraculous birth. The Indians remove the Corn Mother from her niche and set her on a platform. The bells toll. In the balcony the choir sings; each aisle empties before the Corn Mother and everyone streams outside.

Suddenly a gorilla-masked dancer carrying a whip bullies his way through the crowd. How droll he looks. *El Abuelo's* job is to keep order, make sure everyone honors the sacred. He cracks his whip at the dogs; they cringe and scatter. Photography is not allowed; the story went around last year that a couple of *Abuelos* picked up a photographer, confiscated his camera, and dumped him in the Rio Pueblo.

Two men appear bearing flaming torches eight feet high. A step behind them, walking abreast, are four riflemen in moccasins and jeans, their long, black hair in braids or pony tails, the firelight honing the angles of their cheeks. According to anthropologists, in this dramatic collision of Spanish and Indian cultures the rifles symbolize the force used to convert the Indians to Christianity. But their faith submerged into the kivas, deep into the belly of Mother Earth, where it rumbles and prances to this day.

Young girls dance up and down, circling in line, followed by the choir singing their own placid rhythms. Bonfires spring to life as the procession passes; orange flames blaze from yards and rooftops all over the Pueblo. Green piñon crackles; sparks flare and black smoke spirals upward. Across the river firecrackers streak the air with red and gold. The cottonwoods are black silhouettes against the snowy ground. A small plane hums by, red and green lights winking. From the flat housetops draped figures stand motionless, watching.

Masked Matachines dancers in bishop-style hats decked with satin ribbons dance to a Spanish jig played on a fiddle while ankle bells jingle and the air resonates to the deep vibration of the drum. Then comes Corn Mother on her platform beneath a canopy that billows pink and mauve in the sunset. The rifles crack. We fall back laughing, our hearts thudding as small boys scramble for the spent shells.

A colorful sea of spectators sways in the firelight across the frozen field. We say hello to neighbors and embrace old friends as we line up along the return path. I study the faces of the people around us—alive to the drama of the moment, eyes bright with excitement, lips parted, mute with wonder as they watch the sparks twirl overhead.

As the procession returns we edge between the bonfires. One rifleman lights up a cigarette and fires a random shot before they file back into the church. On the bank of the river I turn in slow motion, savoring this medieval drama of fire and ice.

> Now we slide down into darkness
> To touch the hem of light
> Down into icy stillness
> This blue winter night

To celebrate the sacred springs
To light the flame that throbs and sings
To feel the brush of angel wings
In swift, ecstatic flight.

Back home, with a fire crackling in the wood stove and the Christmas tree lights warming the living room, we finished wrapping presents and tucked them under the tree. Then Rachel and I went for a moonlight walk up the hill. We paused at the first switchback to survey the valley, a sprinkling of orange lights in black velvet darkness. I watched her face in profile, the molded curves of cheek and chin, her sensuous mouth, the lines of her white scarf draped around her shoulders.

"I worried about you," she said. "But I won't anymore. You have this—you're in the warm embrace of the land."

"Yes."

She reached for my hand. "I've always been different. I couldn't understand why. But when I come home, I remember. It's this place where I grew up. I have it inside me, only I forget. I feel the power of this valley. I don't know what it is, but it's here. It's magic. As long as I keep in touch with this, I'm okay."

A few days later, as they were packing to leave, Aaron asked, "Will you be lonely?"

I paused beside the kitchen counter, looking up into his brown face. "A little. A little cold, a little hungry, a bit lonely. But that's how I live."

Rachel finished packing first and went out to chop some wood for me. "I want to learn how to do it," she said. "I like the feeling of taking care of you." She was wearing a purple flannel shirt, her auburn hair curling past her waist, bright in the morning sun. Her swing was strong, but sometimes she missed and the log went flying.

I finished washing the breakfast dishes while Brian brought

in split logs and stacked them beside the fireplace. Aaron poked his head out the door. "Hey, that looks like fun." He went out and took the ax from Rachel, chopping with great vigor. I hung in the doorway, watching. "I always liked the sight of you chopping wood," I said. "Out there in the snow in your red and black checked shirt."

"I remember that shirt. My mother bought it for me."

Before I knew it, I had kindling and a neatly-stacked woodpile under the porch. Aaron shook out his arms. "That was exhilarating." The three of them grinned at each other, cheeks rosy.

Hugs and kisses. I followed them to the car and watched as they got in and drove away. I figured they wouldn't notice the tears if I kept grinning and waving.

Daily Bread

I'm restricting my diet so severely that I'm losing energy, getting clumsy. My bank balance has dropped below two hundred and I'm in a low-level panic. I can keep my wood consumption down by living in the two back rooms, stapling plastic over the windows and making heavier curtains. Also, Mara, the owner of Quick Copy, says she'll lend me money if I get stuck. I used to run a typing service for her. I do hate to borrow. I applied there again, but she doesn't need anyone right now.

She took me out to lunch. I talked about breaking up with Aaron and trying to divide the land. She suggested I opt for the house and the land between the ditch and the river, including the orchard, and give up the back hillside. That struck me as a possible solution, but who would want to buy the hillside with building restrictions on it? What could they do with it? The only people who might be interested would be our neighbors who own contiguous pieces of land.

I bought *The Taos News* and scanned the want ads. As usual, pickings in Taos are slim. They need a counter person at Lotaburger, a dishwasher at Doc Martins, a desk clerk at the Quail Ridge Inn. I'm not that desperate yet but I have to hustle. I considered applying at Amigos, the natural food store. The employment office suggested a job working with emotionally disturbed children. The desk clerk job at the Mabel Dodge Luhan House still sounds the best, if I can get it. I'm over-qualified, but they won't know that.

I developed a lot of different skills as administrator of the Unitarian Universalist Church in Boulder; my duties included paying the bills, renting rooms for weddings and receptions, recruiting volunteers, organizing retreats, dinners and rummage sales and producing the monthly newsletter. I was so in love with my job I planted bulbs in the garden, fixed the stained glass window, led support groups, organized services when the minister was out of town, and with his authority I even married two couples. I regularly put in about ten volunteer hours a week.

The only writing I did during those two years was in my journal. When I re-read it I'm struck by my pattern of avoiding the nine-to-five prison, always choosing to write. No wonder I'm having such a *deja vu* feeling. But I knew I had to pay my dues if I was going to get published, win the contest, the grant.

And now? Establish yourself somehow. Don't expect a man to rescue you. I should find a full-time job for about a year so I can pull this place together. But I've lost motivation and energy. Maybe because of the shorter days and the deep cold. I just want to hunker down and read. And write. Fill up the page, keep going. As natural and necessary to me as breathing. But sometimes food and firewood have to come first.

I need to spiff up my résumé. Where to start? I sat down at my desk and chewed on the end of my pen. Should I stress my medical background or my writing skills? In high school I always got As in English, but gravitated toward science because I loved animals and nature. How proud I was when my sister, Betsy, got me my first summer job at the age of fifteen in a lab at the University of Michigan. My duties included fertilizing frog eggs and bleeding rabbits. I could squeeze eggs out of a mama frog without hurting her, but I had a hard time ignoring the baleful red eyes of the rabbits that glared at me as I nicked their ears with a razor blade and stole their blood. I wasn't much on cutting the heads off "sacrificed" frogs either, though I did take some of the legs home for dinner. More often, I let them go in a goldfish pond in the inner courtyard.

On weekends I roamed the woods and lakes of the Pinkney Recreation area twenty miles outside of Ann Arbor or rode my bicycle on the dirt roads around Peach Mountain. Every night after school I rowed our skiff up and down the black Huron River. But in 1958 when Mom and Dad decided to move us back to their hometown of Birmingham fourteen miles outside of Detroit, I fell into a deep depression. Too much concrete and barbed wire, competition and snobbery.

While filling out an application for an advertising job at Chrysler, Dad sank into a depression, too, moaning because he had had forty-seven jobs and didn't have room to list them all. He had a bachelor's degree in English from the University of Michigan, but that didn't translate into a job. His mother said, "At the rate you're going, you're going to end up on a park bench." He rubbed his balding dome. "What are they going to think of someone who's had so many jobs? They'll never hire me."

He was right. But in his day that's what writers were supposed to do—get out there and live so they'd have something to write about.

In my freshman year at Wayne State, while I was living with Grandmother in her stately house on an elm-lined avenue in Birmingham, Dad got an FHA loan and made a down payment on a rinky-dink house in Ferndale a few miles closer to Detroit. To me Motown was like a sooty black spider, slowly sucking us in. Betsy was the only one in the family who was employed. Michigan was in a recession and Mom and Dad had both lost their jobs. When I dropped out of college and came home for Christmas, the family was in crisis. Dad turned to me with a wild-eyed look. "You'd better find a job. This ship is sinking. They're threatening to turn off the gas and the electricity. They don't care if we freeze to death."

Alaska had just opened up for homesteading and Dad was determined to head north, "even if we have to hike up the Al-Can Highway with packs on our backs."

"But, Dad, it's January," I said.

He had accepted a job as a reporter on the *Anchorage News*, but changed his mind when he found out there was no housing. It took about a week for him to bully Betsy into taking over the FHA loan, the car and the furniture payments. Then Mom and Dad signed up to deliver a drive-away car from Detroit to California. With tents and sleeping bags, my younger brother and the dog in tow, they drove to San Francisco, spent the last of their cash and flew to Hawaii. Dad's plan was to camp on the beach and fish for food.

Mom begged me to come, too, but it sounded precarious. I chose to stay with Betsy in Ferndale. I was engaged to my high school sweetheart, Ronnie, who had sold his hubcaps to buy me a diamond ring.

"Get a job," Betsy said. "I need fifteen dollars a month from you to make the mortgage."

"Sha da-da duh/Sha da-da da-da duh/Yip yip yip yip/Yip yip yip yip/Mum mum mum mum mum/Get a job!" I sang. "I will. Give me a chance."

I could type a little, but I didn't know shorthand and wasn't any good at making change. After a couple of weeks of wearing down my heels pursuing jobs I wasn't qualified for, I noticed an ad that said, "Travel to Florida! Join a crew of young women 18-25, wear attractive airline hostess type uniforms to pass out advertising brochures."

"I don't believe it," Betsy said. She warned me about white slavery, but it was one step up from that. Three weeks later I found myself trying to sell magazine subscriptions in bowling alleys and skating rinks in Jacksonville. I wasn't much good at it; the boss called me "One-A-Day." When he announced that we were headed West, I bailed with a girl from Wyandotte. He gave us three dollars apiece and dropped us off at the bus station. We tried to hitchhike home and ended up in jail in Kentucky—but that's another story.

Back in Ferndale with Betsy, I answered an ad for a carhop at the Totem Pole Drive-In on Woodward Avenue. Come rain, sleet or snow, I carried trays on the night shift for twenty-five cents an hour plus tips, and pulled in about forty dollars a week.

In October, when the red leaves were falling, I married Ronnie and he moved in with Betsy and me. He was working for free in his dad's foundry, trying to keep it from going under.

On a wave of optimism, I graduated to an indoor, sit-down job as an information operator at Michigan Bell Telephone Company in Royal Oak. The training was fun, but once I'd learned my way around the directory, my brain went fuzzy. I'd nod off while looking up a number, and wake with a start. My customer light would be on, but I would have no memory of the party to whom I had been speaking.

During my breaks, ensconced on the leather couch in the lounge, I wrote in my spiral notebook a take-off on Zane Grey's romance, "The Call of the Canyon," which grew into my first novella. They called me "girl who writes."

Because I was new, I was forced to work all the holidays. On New Year's Eve when a customer shouted at me, I lost my temper and hung up. My supervisor happened to be monitoring the call. She paused behind me and plugged into my station. "No, don't turn around. Face your board. If you ever—ever!—hang up on a customer again, you will just pick up your purse and walk out of here. Is that understood?"

I nodded; my cheeks burned. I fought down an impulse to do just that. I had a husband to support.

My first resolution on New Year's Day was to find some way to escape from Michigan Bell. We hadn't recovered from the Cuban missile crisis, which threw us all into a panic. People were building bomb shelters in their back yards. I just wanted to flee. I had a yen to see America before they blew it up. Ronnie and I talked about settling in New Mexico or Arizona, buying some land and starting a dude ranch. Ronnie knew how to hunt and fish; he could be a wilderness guide and I'd take the guests horseback riding.

In the spring we bought and fixed up an old Harley-Davidson 80, painted it red and named it Gypsy. In July, with about fifty dollars, an old army tent and bedrolls, we took off on an outdoor adventure, planning to camp out and work our way around the country. I was taking notes for a book I planned to call *Two for the Road*.

In Traverse City we picked cherries with migrant workers from Mexico who could strip the branches twice as fast as we could. In Norwalk, Connecticut, we camped in the woods in the rain until everything we owned was soaking wet. Water was running out of my shoes the morning they hired me to work at a factory inserting blank pages into photo albums. Ronnie got a job in a shoe store.

By October we had fixed up the bike and saved a hundred dollars. We headed south, but the generator gave out on us, then the clutch. Dragging long sacks between our legs, we picked cotton in Texas until our fingers bled. We kept it up until noon, collected eight dollars between us, bought a tank of gas and split.

The going got rough, but we never begged. In a pinch, we collected pop bottles, cashed them in and bought bread and beans. Three days hungry, we sold our blood for five dollars a pint. Afterwards I fainted and wet my pants.

But we were young and I was high on the outdoor life. These were the days before freeways, when the main highway ran right through the middle of every city and Route 66 was a sweet, two-lane blacktop with hills and curves. I clung to Ronnie's back and played "Moon River" on his harmonica; we cheered each time we crossed a state line.

But the bike kept breaking down and Ronnie abandoned it in Albuquerque. I stormed and wept. For me, this was the end of our dream. Ronnie's mother sent bus fare, but I wouldn't go back to sooty old Detroit. We parted in a bus station in Kansas City; I never saw him again.

I went on to Greenwich Village where my favorite cousin, Gretchen, was living the arty life. I took a run-down room in the Broadway Central Hotel and walked eighteen blocks back and forth every day to Macy's, working a temporary job wrapping Christmas presents in the sub-basement.

Over the next three years I sank even lower. I moved to a small town in Maine and married an ex-con named Frenchie, who spent his days in the pool hall and ran up bills all over town. Though he was a gentle guy and a conscientious worker, no one would hire him. Everyone in town knew he had seduced the police chief's daughter and been sent up for four years for statutory rape.

He was handsome, with black eyes, and a sexy smile—until he took out his dentures. Without them, he looked forty, though he only had ten years on me. What was the attraction? He knew how to shoot and trap, canoe and snowshoe. While reading *Wilderness Wife* by Kathrene Sutherland and Gedney Pinkerton, I came up with a different version of the dream I had had with Ronnie: we would save enough money to buy guns, traps and supplies and go live on a lake in the Canadian wilderness.

I grabbed a job as a maid cleaning cabins at Old Orchard Beach, walking eight miles back and forth to work. Finally, I got in at Pepperell Manufacturing Company as a seamstress, binding baby blankets. Every morning we crossed a covered bridge at the entrance of the tall, red brick factory. No one seemed to notice or care that every day the waterfall ran a different color, depending on which dye they were dumping.

I liked the polished hardwood floors, the long windows that let in the sunlight. I was adept at sewing; after a couple of years the workers who collected my blankets from the shaft below were knocking on the floor telling me to slow down. I could tell by touch if I had missed a corner, so I'd prop up a book and read—as long as the boss didn't catch me.

I was twenty-five when Gretchen invited me to a "knock-down, drunken blast" in New Haven. She had married a Yalie who came from a wealthy family. They lived in a cottage with grass and roses and already had a baby. At dawn, sitting under an apple tree reading sonnets to each other, I fell in love with a dark-eyed poet. I dumped Frenchie, filed for a divorce, and two months later moved to Connecticut to be with Frank. He didn't even know I was coming. I blew into town with thirty-five dollars, rented a room that morning across from the Yale dorm on Wall Street, and by late afternoon had grabbed a sewing job at the Gant shirt factory.

A few days after I started at Gant, the city buses went on strike. I had to walk twenty blocks to work and home. Too bad I had sold my three-speed Schwinn. I applied for a job at Yale and was hired as a lab technician to clean cages in a small building called The Mouse House.

When I was kicked upstairs to a lab, I discovered that slicing up and discarding innocent animals was not what I wanted to do with my life. I smuggled out white mice in my purse and let them go in the woods; I pedaled home with pussycat tails dangling from beneath my jacket.

Ever optimistic, I married Frank and moved into his basement apartment. My third mistake. I still didn't want a conventional relationship, and neither did he, but he gave up poetry and took a supervisor's job at a local gun factory. Without malice or forethought, we made each other miserable. His version of it ran: "Love is like a carnival—a lot of bright lights, a dizzy whirl, and then a long line of concessions."

I found a job in the insurance department at Yale-New Haven Hospital. From the safety of my glassed-in Office of Professional Services, I wallowed to my heart's content in the human drama that opened to me in medical charts.

By 1969 I had reached the pinnacle of my career in the medical field—and lost another husband. It was the dawning of the Age of Aquarius. I bought a VW bug, loaded a couple of boxes of my worldly goods and Granddad's leather suitcase with all the travel stickers on it, and hit the road again, heading West.

——— ——— ———

I set aside my résumé and head into the chilly kitchen to heat up some coffee. Unlike Dad, I only have to list my last five jobs—all respectable, each one with a letter of recommendation. I should be able to find something, even in Taos. I haven't had as many jobs as my father, but I have more layers of life experience than Route 66, and I'm so well-traveled you can see the thread in my tread.

——— ——— ———

Shopping at Smith's, I ran into an artist friend, Suann Laskar. We had a long talk in the aisle, leaning on our baskets. Back in the 80s she and I ran the only two typing services in Taos; we handed off jobs to each other.

Suann is a gentle soul with a purity of expression that renders her unique in the modern world. Though she must be close to fifty, she has never been married or had children. She lives alone in Talpa in a three-room house with a wood stove but no plumbing. She bathes at the spa and chops her own wood. She doesn't make enough at typing to support herself. "I take food stamps—a hundred dollars a month. You should get on it, too."

I gave her a wan smile.

She sighed. "It's been a terrible winter. I hate the cold." She described going to Olguín's to beg for sixteen dollars worth of wood. "He wouldn't give it to me. He said, `When are you going to pay it back?' I said, `Monday. You can afford to lend me sixteen dollars. You work here every day.'" She shook her curly head. "I could barely keep from crying in front of him."

Her self-appointed spiritual task is to paint the energy of all twenty-two letters of the Jewish alphabet on four-foot canvasses. "I don't know why I'm doing it or how it will be received."

"Being an unknown artist is like paddling through the Arctic, hoping to sight land," I said.

"Yes. It's taken me five years. I've been studying the Cabala for ten years, but I'm still just a beginner."

"Do you meditate?"

"Yes," she said. "It's helped me break through to another level. But I'm trying to stay here on Earth."

"It's hard to stay present—easy to leave."

"This is true."

"Are you going out with anyone?" I asked, admiring her clear, pale skin and intense, blue eyes.

"I never go out."

"Me either. Don't you get lonely?"

A smile lit her face like the morning sun. "I believe he's out there somewhere. He's looking for me."

I hope she's right. I hope he shows up soon.

As I drove home from town, the fields were burnished gold, the willows red, the bare cottonwood branches like puffs of smoke above the stream. I turned onto the dirt road and crossed the field between twisted cedar posts strung together with barbed wire, over the bridge that spans the gushing, half-frozen waters of the Rio Hondo, up the opposite bank and into my own driveway.

Before the sun set I hurried down to the swing for a whirl through the air, then back up to the house to light a fire and cook some veggies and rice. I slipped into my battered loafers and faded jeans. There's something so comfortable about old clothes that fit like an extra skin.

I woke up feeling depressed. The house looked grungy in the morning sunlight. But the sky was clear and the sunlight brilliant. I started a crock-pot of beans and posole, potatoes, carrots and onions.

I wrote all morning and in the late afternoon took Ocho along while I roller bladed on the lower Hondo road beside the *rio*. The air was clear and an occasional car rumbled past. Every stone—even tiny pebbles—cast long, purple shadows in prickly patterns, like hoarfrost.

Just before sunset I chopped wood for ten minutes. Now I'm lying in bed listening to the fire crackling in the wood stove. So the day is over and I'm not in pain or even much anxiety. I'm carried along by the pleasure of being home.

Today I followed up on phone calls and job leads. I was hoping they would hire me to teach creative writing at the Northern New Mexico Community College in Española, though it would mean a long drive three times a week. Instead, they hired a Ph.D. But they took me on to teach poetry, if I can fill a class. It pays twelve dollars an hour. Tomorrow I'll go apply for whatever I can get.

I also talked to Aaron about dividing the property at the ditch so he could sell the back hillside and get his half of the money out of it. He said he'd think about it.

I called Taos Temps to let them know I'm out here. They said to call back tomorrow morning. I'll go by their office instead. I hate the whole business of trying to sell myself in this town. People who have known me for years give me a blank look: "What do you do?"

It's partly my own fault. I've been a closet novelist for years—never claimed my identity as a writer. For years fighting for the Rio Hondo kept me from being hired at *The Taos News*. The former editor was a staunch friend of the owner of the ski resort.

Last night I dreamed I sat in Granddad's chair, the black walnut one with the curved back. I'd never had the nerve to do it before. The minute I sat down I began to tingle all over. The chair took off and sailed around the room. I was scared, but told myself not to be frightened. "It's magic!" I laughed. Suddenly I was able to control the flight, and brought the chair to an easy landing.

I lay in bed thinking about the dream. He was a journalist, and I dared to sit in his chair. So I got up, went into town and filled out an application at *The Taos News*, then pursued every ad that seemed even remotely appropriate. Left résumés all around and stopped by the Temp Agency. On an impulse I put an ad in the paper offering editing/critiquing—something I'm good at and enjoy. The ad cost seven dollars, which I charged to my credit card.

On the way out of town, I applied at Overland Sheepskin to do sewing. They said come back in the spring. I could be very skinny by spring. At Smith's I ran into another old friend. He asked how long I was staying in Taos. I said, "Till I get a job or starve to death, whichever happens first."

This morning I hiked up into the national forest. Wore myself out. The stock pond is frozen over. It might be fun to skate on when it's solid. Jogging back on the bridle trail, a thought hit me. Why am I always in such a hurry? Through an opening in the trees in a pool of pale sunlight I saw a large, flat stone. I lay back on its smooth surface and gazed up at the sky. No breath of wind stirred the branches. Profound stillness overtook me. This must be how it feels to die, everything stripped bare, just me and the empty vault of heaven. Fear gripped my gut and yanked my limbs taut. I was sinking into the earth, about to be swallowed by the void. Jump up and run!

I sat up, crossed my legs and closed my eyes. Stay with it, stay with it. . . . The familiar meditation pose steadied me. I sat motionless. The silence became me; my breath expanded through every cell. Only in silence can I hear my inner guide.

Snuggles jumped up on the bed and heaved her body into the curve of my stomach this morning. I curled around her, taking comfort in her warmth. At last I got up and poured myself fresh orange juice in my turquoise cup. The juice was a treat. It came free from Amigos Co-op. I noticed a box of shriveled oranges under the counter—mine for the asking. Some were soft and some were hard but when I cut them open, all but two were still edible. I squeezed them into my cup and greedily drank the whole thing down in spite of my cold sore.

I have to call the hospital today to see if they need a back-up medical transcriber. When the children were small I worked for doctors in Taos. My first job in Boulder was as a transcriber at Boulder Community Hospital. The last time I inquired at Holy Cross they were paying transcribers six seventy-five an hour to spend the day in a windowless room under neon lights. I'm one of those people who can't bear to be trapped inside all day, especially under neon lights.

I think of selling one of the Indian pots—and getting taken. I think of panning for gold in the Rio Hondo. But how would I explain where I struck it rich? I answer ads, wash dishes, feed the animals, chop wood, work on my novel, go down to the swing. The sun comes up. The sun goes down. My days run out like sand in the timer.

Aaron says he offered the back hillside to Alan Rose, our neighbor at the top of the hill. Alan said he might be interested in buying a parcel to the south to protect his privacy. How much is a parcel? Could he be persuaded to buy the whole hillside, all twenty acres?

Part of me says you can't hang onto the land forever—take the money and run. But where? I could buy a sloop and sail the Caribbean. Lost at sea.

My inner voice whispers, "This is a test. Don't make decisions based on anger or fear. You don't have to agree to anything you don't want. But don't get Aaron's back up, either. Forget the transient factors, the financial struggle, the physical struggle. Being lonely. All this will change, but the land stays."

The house is freezing. I woke at dawn with the cat walking on my head and couldn't get back to sleep. I hopped in the shower and ran out the whole tank of hot water. The day was cold and sharp and clear, except for the mist of wood smoke that drifted over the treetops this morning. I love the soft winter colors, the faded yellow of the chamisa, the tawny fields and ditches lined with vibrant willows, some vermilion and some like flame, the smoky branches of the cottonwoods leading the eye upward to mountains bright with snow.

I finally got around to winterizing, starting with insulation around the bedroom windows. I stuffed the cracks around the back door with wads of batting and nailed it shut, but the walls are so cold if I let the fire die within ten minutes the warmth evaporates and a chill settles over the room.

Learned Hand says: "What we do for eight hours a day, five days a week, more or less, is bound to have a profound impact on our sense of identity and self-esteem. The quality of our lives in large part depends on the quality of our work."

Our job defines who we are, gives us companionship, status and self-esteem that come from "a sense of competency and producing something valued by others," he says. "A person with high self-esteem is someone who has a high estimation of his own value and finds that others agree."

But what if she's a novelist and her books don't sell? Better get a day job. Right now my self-esteem depends on how long I can hold out here alone.

It all ganged up on me today—the cold, the loneliness, the feeling that nobody really needs me or wants me here. Fatigue, my cracked lips and cold sores. Some residual anger at Aaron. He's making more money than he's ever made in his life and I have to pay him two hundred and fifty a month to live in my own house. I'm feeling agitated over everything, wondering why I fight so hard to live in rural poverty. Maybe I should just give up. It would make my life a lot easier. My thoughts deteriorated into wishing my rich aunt would die and leave me some money. Only I don't have a rich aunt. Life is not a direct line from beginning to climax, but a circling, circling. I've got to pull out of this. This is my daily mantra: Please, Lord, send me meaningful work. And give me enough time and energy to complete my writing.

Spent all morning typing up queries to various magazines about article proposals. In the afternoon I went down to the river, even took my journal, but forgot a pen. The sun was shining through the Apache plumes on the trees, illuminating their fibers with a glossy fire. I perched on the swing, closed my eyes, felt the sun on my face and watched the show behind my eyelids, dashes of light, red and green, deep purple. I took comfort in pale sunlight on smooth alder trunks, bright rose hips on the tips of the briars. The banks of the stream are rimmed with ice. The water is clear but the rocks are turning mossy again.

This evening another spectacular sunset. The air was so clear the colors were vibrant—peach and violet, rolling layers of purple clouds rimmed with flame. I lit the stove in the living room, opened the doors and sat a long time enjoying the heat, watching the hollow cave of embers where the flames licked blue on the underside of the log.

Got a call from Taos Temp. How soon could I get there? In half an hour, I said. And did. On the highway I picked up a young couple. They had made willow baskets and sage sticks and were taking them to Taos to sell. The young woman was wearing a hand-crocheted hat, several layers of sweaters and a long skirt. Her partner was a bearded fellow in overalls with muddy boots, but they both looked presentable.

At Taos Temp they sent me to a lawyer's office to work for three hours. The Windows program was 5.2, a little different from the ones I know, but I figured it out. The boss asked me to come back tomorrow. I said I would.

Coming home I picked up the basket folks again and gave them a ride to lower Hondo. It would have been a long, cold walk from Herb's Lounge. They were tired but happy—they had sold everything.

Today a truck pulled up. I recognized the staunch figure, the sunglasses and camouflage. Eloy. I gave him a big hug. He sat with me in the kitchen drinking hot chocolate while we caught up. He's been working hard on his house, has the electricity in and storm windows. He sharpened my ax. That helps.

Today Eloy brought me a bag of fresh trout. We talked a long time about jobs and money. He's got it all figured out. His yearlings are worth about five hundred apiece. "If hard times came, I could always sell one."

He says he makes about two hundred and fifty a day taking people fishing at Eagle Nest. He's thinking of going into landscaping in the spring. "I never have any money because I spend it all on building my house and buying land. What good would it do me sitting in the bank? Besides, they wouldn't lend me five thousand to get my guide business started, so the heck with them."

I received a paycheck from Taos Temps for twenty-four dollars and a belated Christmas check from Aaron's father for fifty. He says I will always be part of the family. I sat right down to compose a thank you note, then bicycled to the post office to mail it. It's uphill all the way home. I pushed the pedals down and around, chanting under my breath, "I think I can, I think I can, I think I can!"

Dogs and Sheep

*B*etsy called to say hello. She asked if I was working and how much money did I have left and what was I going to do? "You'd better get some kind of a job."

A déjà vu feeling swept over me. "Sha da-da duh!" I sang. "I'm trying. I made nine dollars an hour as a medical transcriber at Boulder Community Hospital, but in Taos I can't get a job as a receptionist at the vet's for four dollars and thirty cents an hour, though he's my vet and I almost begged him."

"How's the economy?"

I said in an ironic tone, "I don't participate in it. People just give me food because I'm living this spiritual life."

Her tone was solemn. "I'm not telling you how to live your life, but if it was me, I'd go live somewhere else."

"I hate moving. I have to take a stand."

She said she was sending me twenty-five dollars. I demurred, but that never gets me anywhere. I feel like such a bum. The good news is, I checked with the editor of "Tempo," the art section of *The Taos News*, to see if she needed freelancers. She sent me out on an assignment to cover an art opening at Westwind Gallery. The paper only pays a dollar an inch, but the editor wants about forty inches. This should be fun.

I'm nursing my knee. I whacked myself with the ax. It didn't cut my pants, but I have a bruise. I slept with the heating pad on it last night. I couldn't dance for exercise, so I decided to go roller blading beside the Rio Hondo. Traffic on the road is thin as it runs through the lower end of the valley, past the one-room post office, Tito's grocery store and the elementary school. I pass a handful of buffalo with big, dark heads, the rusty Model-T Ford, then the Varellas' house under the silver poplars, down through the wet open meadows. The old-timers say there was nothing at this end of the valley but marshes, that it was so wet a cow could sink up to its stomach in mud.

The Varella compound was the last place I stopped the day I went door-to-door with petitions for the Rio Hondo. Their houses were clustered together behind a gate on the other side of the river. A small flock of sheep was grazing in the yard. Nobody seemed to be around. I knocked on the door of the largest house. A woman wearing a white apron opened the door. She invited me to sit at the kitchen table and offered me coffee from an enamel pot on top of the wood stove.

Her face was round, her soft gray hair tied back at her neck. Her hands were white with flour. She went on kneading her bread dough as I ran through my spiel about the Rio Hondo and the sewage treatment plant. On the other side of the table an old man was tipped back in his chair, leaning against the wall, snoring lightly.

After awhile he woke, smiled at me from under his white mustache, got out his catalog and offered to sell me a new pair of shoes. "They last forever," he said.

I was so enchanted by their innate courtesy, overwhelmed by the smell of fresh bread, that I ordered a pair of loafers. The materials were all man-made, and he was right—they never did wear out. I finally gave them away because, after five years, I had grown tired of them.

I drove to the end of the valley where the *acequia* rejoins the river and the watercress grows darkly green. George Baca, Consuelo's husband said, "In the winter that was the only salad we had. We used to eat it with vinegar and olive oil." I hadn't had a salad in awhile; I'd pick some watercress on the way home.

It was a beautiful morning, cold and sunny. I had brought Ocho and Dayglow, a neighbor's dog who sometimes came over to play with mine. Should I put them both on a leash? What if we saw sheep? The Varella flocks weren't usually close to the road, and I wasn't likely to see any others.

Only a handful of families in the valley still raised sheep. Too bad. For generations sheep had been part of their culture. The Spanish Conquistadors brought large herds of *churro* sheep with them from Mexico. Today *churros* are considered a rare breed.

Almost every year *The Taos News* ran a story about sheep that had been attacked by a pack of dogs. I recalled a photo of what looked like a dirty bag of wool lying in a dark pool of blood. Nearby, a dog lay in its own blood, too, with the grieving owner down on one knee. Poor guy.

I laced up my roller blades and headed east, pushing uphill. The dogs took off ahead of me, Dayglow in the lead. As I came abreast of the Varella compound, I was alarmed by the sight of wooly shapes huddled together in the yard.

Dayglow's ears went up. He scooched under the fence and dashed across the field. Luckily, Ocho was too fat to squeeze under. She cast back and forth, trying to find another opening. I whistled frantically but Dayglow disappeared around the corner of the house. I couldn't chase him because of my skates. A feeling of panic clutched my gut. "Damn!" I cringed, waiting for the blast of a gun.

Ocho tried to flatten herself under the fence where a brook ran through. "Come back!" I screamed. For once, she obeyed. I grabbed her by the collar and skated back to the car. That's right, save your own dog first.

I pushed her into the back, jumped behind the wheel, tore off my skates and sped to the Varellas' fields. I hopped into my boots, laces trailing, ducked between the barbed wire and ran toward Dayglow. A sheep was down beside the fence. Wool was flying through the air. My God! He's already eating it.

I caught the dog by the scruff of the neck. The sheep was lying motionless on its side, legs thrust out stiff. Its eyes were open and it was still breathing but its stomach and front leg were bright with blood. "Bad dog! Bad!"

In half a minute I dragged that fifty-pound animal across the field and over two fences without letting go of him. He didn't let out a whimper. My thoughts whirled like flies in a lampshade. No one is home or Dayglow would be dead by now. A sheep must cost what—forty dollars? Fifty? A hundred? It's dead. Or soon will be. I could get in the car and drive away. Hit and run?

I reached the gate. No. You have to go back and look at it, see if there's anything you can do. Leave a note, at least. As I dropped the chain on the gate a pickup turned into the driveway with two of the Varella men in the front seat. They rolled down the window and stared. I threw up one hand. "This dog was after your sheep, but I stopped him." Like I was the hero of the day.

Panting, I locked Dayglow in the car and ran back. The two men stood over the sheep, arms crossed, shaking their heads. The sheep was trembling. I squatted down and stroked its nose. Its eye was a pale yellow-green; it smelled of hay. Its swollen sides declared that it was female, and pregnant.

"I'm so sorry! I'm so very sorry." Tears ran down my face. These guys needed a weeping woman on top of a bleeding sheep? I smeared the tears away.

"A pack of dogs killed seventeen of my brother's sheep last week," the tall one said. "We shot four of those dogs."

The other one nodded. "That dog should be shot right now.

Once they've gone after sheep they'll do it again. You're going to have to pay for her."

An older man came out of one of the houses. He was handsome, with a mustache and clear brown eyes. Paul Varella.

I looked up at him. "You the owner?"

He nodded, asked where I lived, whose dog it was. I said Dayglow belonged to a neighbor—I had brought him along for a walk. "I feel like an idiot. I should have brought the leash, but didn't know what he'd do."

Paul shook his head. "That sheep was worth about a hundred dollars. She was going to give birth in a couple of days. There's probably twins inside her."

I sat down beside her, lifted her front leg and examined her belly. Dayglow had exposed a bald spot the size of my hand. I couldn't see any puncture wounds and there were no guts hanging out, but what was happening on the side she was lying on? A tick wandered around the bald spot. I pinched it off. My hands were red with blood.

"She can't get up," Paul said.

"She's shaking all over. She's in shock."

He tried to roll her over onto her belly, but she just lay there. "Sheep are awfully stupid."

"So are some people," I muttered. I lay my hand on her tight belly. In a minute I felt the knob of a leg or a nose stir against my palm. "The babies are still alive. She's not having contractions. I used to work in a lab. Let me see what I can do. If you bring some warm water and soap, I'll wash her off."

The men gawked at me, then disappeared into the house. While they were gone I uttered a fierce prayer to be able to save this sheep and her babies. Paul came back with a plastic bucket of soapy water, one of cool rinse water and a clean rag. The ewe trembled even more violently as I washed the blood away. All I could find was the small red curve of a bite on the inside of her leg at the hock.

"That's the worst place to get cut," Paul said. "For some reason their legs stiffen up afterward and they can't walk." He passed behind her and stared, hands in his pockets. "Something's wrong down here. Her insides are hanging out. She's probably going to have the lambs right here on the ground."

I was afraid to look. A tube of pink satin flesh protruded about six inches into the frigid air. She was losing body heat. I had had a partial prolapse of the uterus before my hysterectomy and I knew what to do. My hands were already clean, so I gently grasped her vagina and pushed it back inside. It slid out again. The second time I pushed my whole hand up into her smooth, warm flesh. Never dreamed I'd get so intimate with a sheep.

Startled, her head came up and she rolled onto her stomach. I sat beside her and held it in for about ten minutes while Paul squatted and stroked her nose. "I'll take her to the vet if you can lift her into my car," I said. "Or if you want to take her yourself, I'll pay for it."

"Whatever you want to do. We just raise them for our own use."

"I know. That makes me feel even worse. I really apologize. I know better. I've lived around here a long time."

But reading about dogs killing sheep is not the same as sitting on the ground holding a ewe's vagina in place, praying it won't abort.

A flock of blackbirds swarmed into the lower branches of the silver poplar. We were both silent, watching them, listening to them squeak like untuned violins.

"Isn't it a little early in the year for lambing?" I asked.

He nodded. "It's my fault. I didn't take the ram off them. I mean—I didn't separate them."

When I removed my hand the vagina protruded only a couple of inches. I caught a deep breath. "While that's stable I'll take the dogs home. I'll come right back to take her to the vet."

I ran to the car. The windows were steamed up and dripping

with dog breath. I rushed home. The nearest vet was Ivan Schroeder, seven miles away. I called to tell him I was coming and to ask for advice. He said to wash the wounds with soap and warm water and push the vagina back in, that he could stitch any cuts. "If you bring it in and I do an IV and all that it will end up costing far more than a hundred."

I told him I hadn't noticed any bleeding on the vagina. "The cuts on her leg look minor. It's the prolapse I'm worried about."

"Keep pushing it back in, watch her like a hawk and make sure she's eating."

"Will it prolapse again when she gives birth?"

"It won't help. You might want to get some antibiotics for the bites."

"How much?"

"About fifteen."

I could cover it with my first free-lancing check. "I'll be in."

I rushed back to the scene of the crime. Paul was still squatting beside the ewe. Startled by my quick moves, she scrambled to her feet. Her vagina whooshed in. A bit shaky, she trotted off along the fence. Paul and I watched her disappear around the corner of the house as she made her way back to the herd. I was ready to shout hooray but Paul said, "The next thing we have to worry about is infection."

"I'll go get the antibiotics. Do you know how to give them?"

"I've done it before. I can manage it on Tuesday because I have the day off but the other days I have to be to work by eight. Can you do it?"

"Sure." But could I? I had given shots to mice in the lab at Yale. Not the same thing. "I have the time. I'm looking for work."

"Jobs are hard to find right now."

"No kidding."

As I headed for the car I called back over my shoulder, "Thanks for not yelling a me."

He laughed. "But if Alex Romero finds out, he'll come after that dog and shoot it."

As I barreled in the door, Ivan gave me a searching look. He handed me a can of spray disinfectant for the bites, two dollars off because he had already used it a couple of times. I thanked him. Then two new syringes. "Give her the shot in the back of the thigh. It's not hard."

Not when you've done it a few times, I suppose.

"You might have to cut away the wool and shave the spot."

"Uh-huh." But the wool is three inches thick. The idea of shaving a spot, even the size of a silver dollar, off a sheep's thigh while she struggles to get away. . . .

"Try not to hit the sciatic nerve that runs along the back of the leg," he continued. "The skin is about an inch thick; it doesn't do any good to get the shot in there because it won't diffuse. You have to pinch up the muscle." He pinched my triceps. "Pull the syringe back to make sure you haven't hit a blood vessel. Then plunge it and pull it out." He pressed his thumb to the imaginary puncture wound on my arm. Deft. Finished.

Sure—if it's a very passive sheep.

"Soak the needles in alcohol between use."

"Right."

I drove back to Hondo, knocked at the door and handed Paul the syringes, spray and the bottle of liquid penicillin. "How's she doing?"

"She's looking pretty sad but otherwise seems okay. Can you come over in the morning, Wednesday through Sunday, and give the shots?"

"Sure."

He showed me the corral in back of the house where the sheep would be penned. There was a roof over one end of it. It would be dark. He followed my thoughts. "I'll put an orange ribbon on her."

I had to talk to Chris, the man who owned Dayglow, ask him to come and help hold the ewe. When I showed up at his door with the bad news he said he had to be to work at eight, too, but he could do it at seven if I could get up that early. He admitted this wasn't the first time Dayglow had gone after sheep. "But when he catches them he doesn't know what to do. The first time he did it I beat him senseless."

"I wish you'd told me."

"I should have. Sorry."

"So that didn't work. Violence only begets more violence."

He nodded. "I was raised on it. That's why I left home at sixteen. That's why I became an alcoholic. I guess it's time to try something else."

I woke up at five the next morning trying to imagine how to pin a pregnant sheep. Where do I get a grip—without squeezing the babies out? By the faint light of dawn I washed my face and filled a plastic bag with alcohol, paper towels, scissors, my razor and a flashlight.

I was about to call Chris when the phone rang. It was Mrs. Varella: "My husband told me to call you not to come. He already shot the sheep."

"What?" My hand flew to my chest. "Shot her?"

"He already did it. He said she was too hard to get into the corral—'I'd better do it myself.'"

"He gave her the shot?"

"Yes."

I laughed with relief. "*Bueno.* Thanks—thanks for calling."

When I checked back the next day, Paul told me the ewe had delivered two live lambs without any difficulty.

"That's great."

"But she lay on one of them and crushed it."

168 ————

"Oh! I'm sorry." One spindly-legged lamb, gone from the world. But it might have been two."

"It's not your fault," he said. "Sheep are stupid."

"So I hear."

"Her leg didn't swell up. She seems to be doing fine. Thanks for helping out."

"I'm sorry I caused you so much trouble."

These last few days the light has been lucid; tree shadows across the tarmac are thin and tremulous; the sky is cloudless, the sun hot. Hollyhock leaves are curling up green at the bottoms of the stalks and I was buzzed by a yellow jacket.

I left the dog at home and peddled slowly down to lower Hondo. The Varellas' sheep were bunched up in a field across the road. I spotted my ewe by her orange ribbon. She paused a moment to regard me with one pale green eye. A black lamb nudged her udder, then trotted after her as she wandered off to graze on spears of new grass.

High above I heard strange, rattling cries. A huge flock of birds must be flying north. I stood still, staring up into the blank sky. The stream of sound went on for over two minutes, and suddenly I knew what it was. The annual migration of sandhill cranes, flying so high I couldn't see them.

I inhaled the soft air and let out a sigh. Spring!

The Antler

*M*y artist friends, Jan and Jim, are down from Boulder to visit me for a few days. They get up early and we have breakfast together. Then they set up their easels in the yard and paint their way around the house, from one view to another. It's wonderful seeing my humble adobe transcend on canvas. They portray it the way I feel it.

Spent most of yesterday in the studio working on my novel, or, to be honest, wrestling with creative tension, while Jan and Jim painted near the open door. We met sporadically in the kitchen over food. It's been fun having them around. Tomorrow morning they're heading out for Canyonlands.

Aaron called and we argued about the sale of the land. He said, "Nobody wants that rocky hillside. I offered it to the Cohns, but they're not interested. Then I offered it to Steve Brody, but he's selling off pieces right now." Steve was our neighbor to the east.

"What about Alan? Maybe I should go up and talk to him."

"I called him last week. When I told him how much I wanted, he said no." Long pause. "I'm not taking less than my half is worth." He said if I want to keep the house I can buy him out, but I'd have to get my own financing. I've never borrowed money in my life.

What would I use for collateral? He said, "I don't want to have you owe me a thousand dollars a month for the rest of my life. What would be my recourse if you missed a payment?"

He had a point, but I felt crushed and angry. Feeling a need to connect with people on a spiritual level, I attended Unity Church this morning. The minister talked about surrendering our ego, our desire and our fear in order to let God lead us so that we can follow in trust and faith. To truly surrender our lives and see how much better it gets. He was quite eloquent; I smiled with pleasure.

I drove home slowly through the spring landscape, the weeping willows deep yellow against tall dark mountains streaked with snow, a surrealistic blaze of white against a flat, blue sky. The fields are emerald with thousands of yellow dandelions like little lights in the grass. What a day! I decided to walk back to Lobo Creek. Chris told me he had felt the wind blowing up through the rocks from a cave near a big ponderosa pine. He thought there might be a gold deposit and told me what to look for—black sand in the creek bed.

Gold. Lobo Creek runs down from Gold Hill. They say that Simeon Turley had a bag of gold, but he was massacred during the Taos Pueblo uprising along with most of the other white men in the area including the American Territorial Governor Charles Bent. When a drunken mob attacked and burned Turley's whiskey mill, hidden by a cloud of black smoke, he rushed out the back door. Did he grab the gold from its hiding place? Or was it buried somewhere else?

Twelve years ago a man came by with a metal detector searching through the fields at the head of our valley but never found anything. With my head full of fantasies, I too went searching for the gold. What would it be like to be suddenly rich? Would I have to stake a claim? Or would it belong to the property owner? My sudden wealth would arouse *envidia*, envy, in the village. I'd have to share.

The first thing I'd do, of course, would be to buy out Aaron's half of the property. Then a reliable car. Then a trust fund for the kids' college. Then, then. . . .

    I followed a thin deer trail over the top of the mesa and down the other side until I emerged in a wild, narrow canyon with three huge ponderosas. I sat on a boulder by the side of the dry streambed and felt the silence of many small lives waiting for me to pass.

    I wandered up the sandy streambed. Around a bend under a pine tree I caught sight of something I could hardly believe—the white curves of a huge antler lying on a bed of pine needles as if an elk had bowed his head and laid his heavy burden down. I approached it in awe. Overhead, a black turkey vulture trailed ragged wing feathers, soaring on the wind. I had a sense of some great honor being conferred on me.

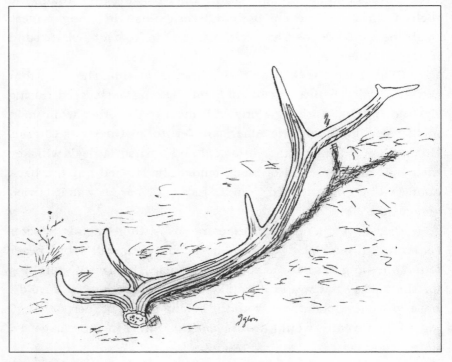

The Antler

I imagined taking the antler home—of course I wanted to. I'd never found anything so beautiful. It must be worth money—I remembered a truck outside of Cimmaron with a sign saying they bought antlers and bones. Sixty dollars? Seventy? A hundred? Not that I'd sell it.

I thought of what I could trade it for and all the people I could give it to. In the end none of that felt right. I had to let it go. Not to see if it came back—just let it go, leave it. For awhile. It looked so natural and right in its bed of brown needles and oak leaves.

I measured it with my arms as wide as I could stretch, left fingers on the base and right fingers on the tip. I counted six points. I examined the porous, bony end that had detached from the elk's head. I stroked its grooved surface, ran my hands over the cool, ivory-colored tips.

Still jangled by the argument with Aaron, I prayed to be as graceful, strong and pure as this antler, to be free, to have myself, to follow my path, surrender my life. For me, this was a test. If I couldn't walk away from this antler, how could I let go of the land, the life we once had together?

I began to understand why spiritual people like Pema Chödrön can't own anything—because we're repeatedly dragged back to defend it, fear for it, and care for it. Pema was never deeply attached to this house when she lived here with her two children as Aaron's first wife. But she was desperately attached to Aaron. It took her a long time to let go of him and find her own center. I prayed for the strength to let go of Aaron entirely, of wanting him, judging him, feeling bitter about the past, and blaming him. And with it, to surrender my green pastures, my rushing waters? Who could take better care of the land than God?

"If you want me to stay here, make it possible. If not, I'll go. It's up to you," I said. I decided to start looking for land at the other end of the valley. To tell Aaron that's what I'm doing and let him off the hook about financing me. I can do it myself. Or not. There is nothing more important than our relationship. The bond of family between us is real and will always be there no matter what.

Ocho barked. I heard voices. I snatched the antler and scrambled up the side of the hill into the woods. I squatted down behind a tree and sat looking at what I had in my hands, chagrinned. So much for letting go. I imagined it on the mantle. Losing its magic. Gathering dust. If I didn't take it someone else would. I looked around for a less obvious place to stash it. But in the end I laid it back under the tree where it belonged.

I made up my mind not to tell anyone about the antler, to come back in a week and, if it was still there, to take it home. The decision felt clean, pure and powerful.

When I got home I called Aaron and told him what I had decided. He was relieved, glad I had called back. When I said I'd always love him no matter what, that we'd always be family, his voice faltered and tears welled up in my eyes.

It snowed in the night. The air was nippy, the sky scoured clean, the land sparkling. I thought of the antler lying under the tree and wondered if there was snow on it. All day the thought of my antler was like sunlight inside me. I wanted it in my hands. I had let it go. But I could take it back. I could run back there and take a picture—at least I'd have that.

I pulled on my boots, called Ocho and bounded up the hill as fast as I could go. Soon I was out of breath and my throat hurt. I kept on at a wild pace until I had to force myself to slow down. I trotted down to the streambed feeling as light as Rima in *Green Mansions*. Dry oak leaves scuttled across the sand. Purple spring flowers called to me as I rushed on.

I found my antler still lying in its bed of brown pine needles. I knelt and thanked the powers, caught my breath, then took two pictures to capture the elegance of it. I sat cross-legged in meditation. The wind felt cool on my cheek.

Total surrender means not going back on it. An hour later I

rose and came home feeling pleased to have such a great secret, to hold it in the stillness of my heart.

——— ——— ———

Around four-thirty Eloy stopped by. We sat on a log by the stream, talking. I told him I had found something really beautiful. "An antler," he said.

"I'll show you."

"Let's go right now."

On the way I tried to explain what it meant to me. "I have to learn how to let life guide me."

He nodded and pointed out things along the trail, the track of the elk, which looks like a small cow, then an oval depression in the grass under a tree where the deer had bedded down. A dried-out rope of rabbit and deer hair. "Coyote scat," he said. He picked it up between two sticks. "This is how the Chinese invented chopsticks."

I led him to my spot, sure that the antler would still be there. It was. We sat beside it. He wouldn't touch it. "All antlers are sacred," he said. "I would never sell one." He told me how he had found his first antler. He had been bow hunting in an area where his brothers said there weren't any elk. "I had seen an elk that morning but I didn't shoot it. I always let the first one go—fish or deer or rabbit. The second one was too far away. Elk are very heavy. You need a horse to bring them down the mountain. I was disappointed. Then I found the antler and I felt proud and special. At least I could prove to my brothers that there were elk in that canyon."

He warned me that people were out turkey hunting and looking for antlers right now. "Antlers aren't that easy to find," he said. "That's a nice one. They come a lot bigger. Every year they grow bigger horns with more points. I think they shed them because they need a break just like people do. If you want this antler, you should take it."

"What if nobody takes it?"

He smiled. "Maybe a porcupine will eat it."

I invited him to meditate with me. We sat in silence for a long time listening to the wind, a woodpecker tapping at a tree, the dog panting and whining. Before we left he said if I wanted to protect the antler I should make a circle around it. I walked around it three times, then turned away.

This morning it snowed again. I was happy to spend the day quietly at home. But around two o'clock I began to feel anxious about the antler. Its energy was leaving me. Something said, "If you want it, you'd better go get it." I fought down the feeling for about an hour. It was cold, gloomy, and I didn't feel like going anywhere. By three o'clock the feeling was so strong that I found myself lacing up my boots. Not that I was going to bring the antler home. I just wanted to touch it again.

I set out with the dog and twenty minutes later came to the ponderosas. Something had shifted. Before I reached my sacred place I could feel that the antler was gone. I looked around in the brush but I knew I wouldn't find it. Someone else had carried off my treasure to lie on his or her mantle and gather dust. I sank down, heavy with disappointment, a dark hollow of loss. So what's the lesson here? That I can't accept what life offers?

I meditated for an hour. Feeling more present, I climbed the mesa and headed home. Maybe the lesson was not about letting go; maybe it was about holding on.

I dreamed I was dancing through the village with the antler balanced on my head. I touched crying children and they grew quiet. I flew away over the earth, free.

Sin Agua, No Hay Vida
Without water, there is no life

*W*hat does it take to bring together people of diverse cultures and backgrounds? Sometimes hardscrabble necessity. When it comes to maintaining the *acequias*, there's nothing like two days of unrelenting labor to smooth the edges of your diversity.

Preparation for ditch cleaning usually began in March with a meeting of all the landowners in the cafeteria at the elementary school. We signed in and sat at tables with attached benches, under the harsh neon lights, nodding to friends and neighbors. Flanked by two of his sturdy brothers, Eloy lounged at the back table. He smiled at me, but he was shy in public and wouldn't come over to say hello.

The room grew silent as Ted Green reported how much they had spent this year in headgate repairs, and urged everyone who hadn't paid their ditch fees to cough up. Year after year, the same issues arose. *Parciantes*, landowners with water rights, complained that Valdez took so much of the water that there was only a trickle left for us. Historically, Arroyo Hondo water rights took precedence over Valdez, but they were upstream, and they received the water first.

Our *acequia*, the *Atalaya*, was the longest in the valley and had the fewest people living on it. Every year it was a struggle to recruit enough of a crew to complete the necessary labor. If you don't work or send someone to work in your place, you have to pay a fine. The usual argument broke out about which end of the ditch to start on. Those at the lower end complained that when we started at the top, the crew never had enough time or energy to do a good job by the time they reached the bottom. But Armando pointed out that if we didn't clean the top, nobody would have water. I suggested that we start at alternate ends in alternate years; to my surprise, the motion passed unanimously.

The Zamoras were the largest landowners in the valley, with a hundred and fifty acres at the tail end of the *acequia*. They still ran a small herd of cattle and grew alfalfa and hay to feed them, but they were barely making it. Armando worked for the highway department while he farmed his fifty acres and irrigated on a regular basis. The rest of the water went to various *parciantes'* fields, gardens, yards and domestic animals.

Connie Zamora couldn't attend the meeting, but her sister Contenta had no trouble making her voice heard. The eldest in a family of four girls, Contenta had become the son her father never had. She was short, stocky and vigorous. "My family is willing to pay minimum wage to at least five men or teens," she said, "but nobody wants to work anymore."

I offered to put an ad in the paper and they took me up on it. Contenta said in a fierce tone, "We don't want anyone who's been drinking."

"No drunks," I agreed. Again we discussed the option of using a ditch witch to cut back the banks and willows, but in the end we agreed that the machine couldn't do the same job that we did with clippers, rakes and shovels.

Eloy and two of his brothers were assigned to cut willows with the electric saw a few days ahead of ditch cleaning, and the rest of us would rake the cuttings when we came through. The willows are always a problem. For some reason they're especially thick along my property.

I was the only woman to work on the *Atalaya* back in the 70s when the crew was traditionally made up of middle-aged Hispano men. The women stayed home and cooked big suppers for the men. Wielding a carving knife with a serrated edge, I jumped in beside Aaron and hacked at willows until the blade snapped.

Over the years a few more women came on board. The men accepted us when they saw we could work just as long and hard as they could without fainting.

Ditch cleaning day dawned warm and clear. I slid into my grungy jeans and searched through the cupboard for my gardening gloves. I loaded my shovel in the back of the car and drove up to the highway. Battered pickups were parked nose-to-nose beside the road. The men sat on the hoods of their trucks or gathered in small groups, talking quietly, their eyes lit as if they had come to party. New arrivals were greeted with handshakes, back slaps and friendly grins. "*¿Cómo estás, mi amigo?*"

The answer was usually: "*Bien. ¿Y tú?*"

I was assigned to a work crew and we set out for the west end of the ditch. I threw myself into it like I do, and soon had to sneak off into the chamisa and trade my sweatshirt for an old cotton shirt of Jack's. Jack was a small, well-made man, not much taller than I. Against the clear morning sky, his profile looked clean and precise as if it had been chiseled out of marble—a long straight nose and neatly-clipped white beard. He and Anna owned forty acres at the far end of the valley where they had lived for thirty years. She would take his place in the afternoon.

Trailing behind the middle-aged males came a couple of wiry, Spanish-speaking elders and three teen-aged boys who were already hooked into their Walkmans. I was surprised to see Sean Buckingham, an aristocratic businessman from the other end of the valley, looking dapper in his felt hat. Surely he could afford to hire someone to work for him.

As we cleaned and widened the ditch, shoveling out stones

and clumps of clay, he told me about his Christmas tree farm in North Carolina, how he had harvested and sold up to eight hundred trees per season. "From the field to the customer, you have to pick up and put down every tree eight times," he said.

I was amused by the way his faintly English accent slipped into a country slur as the day wore on. He fell to using expressions like "critters" and "a piece of work." His description of the life he had lived on his tree farm changed the image I had of him as a self-styled country squire. "I've worked hard all my life," he said. "I started pumping gas after school when I was thirteen."

In silence we listened to him talk about his conflicts with his mother. "She was one of the steel magnolias. The only way I could prove myself was by working." He proved himself to his Hondo neighbors the same way.

Emilio followed close behind me all day, ogling my ass. He was a rakish fellow with a bulging beer belly, red-eyed from a Friday-night bout. When I dropped behind him, he stepped aside to let "the young lady pass."

I snorted. "I'm an old bag."

"You're in pretty good shape."

"A compliment!"

Around ten o'clock we took our first break. Freddie, a wiry Anglo in "airborne" fatigues, sat cleaning his shovel. Emilio said, "Is that how you cleaned your gun in `Nam?"

He frowned and stared at his boots. "We never called it a gun. A rifle. Or a piece. Or sometimes even a deer." He glanced at me. "Where's Rachel? I thought she'd be here this year."

"She's in college, studying psychology up in Boulder."

He frowned. "Oh, don't start telling me about the dysfunctional Taos male."

"Okay. A horse walked into the bar and the bartender said, 'Why the long face?'"

As we reached the highway I caught a glimpse of Eloy and his brother Marty wielding electric saws. The willows flew. They had started at the top of the ditch. "How many men do they have up there?" Freddie asked.

"Four," Emilio said, "but those Mascareñas brothers are worth ten each."

When we peered into the culvert that crossed under the highway we found it completely blocked by beaver dams. It stank of mold and rotting vegetation. No one volunteered to crawl in there in the dark and maybe confront an angry beaver. They chipped away at it from both ends while the rest of us went on.

We quit for lunch and came back at one. Our backs and arms were sore from wielding shovels, tossing stones. Blisters broke on my palms from raking willows. As the afternoon dragged on, the sweat poured down our cheeks and we paused more often to gulp the lukewarm water from our canteens.

The last hour was the worst. Dust dried our throats; weeds itched under our collars and down our shirts. With one eye on our watches, we stumbled and faltered. We had forgotten the why of it.

"It's like purgatory," Freddie said.

"You mean hell?" Emilio laughed. "Yeah, I can agree with that."

"No, purgatory. It's never gonna end."

I offered my young friend Karen six bucks an hour to clean the ditch with me on Sunday. She hitchhiked to work every day and I picked her up whenever I saw her. She was tall and lanky and looked as strong as some of the men; I thought she might enjoy the novelty of working in community. She came by the house wearing blue jeans and a sweatshirt, but no hat, though I offered her one of mine.

I was better prepared than I had been on Saturday. I carried a bottle of water, changed my billed cap to a straw hat and traded in my shovel for a rake and clippers. We started at the top of the ditch and worked our way down to the highway. It felt good to have help as we shoveled and cleaned the section that crossed our land. I showed them the muskrat holes and they stuffed them with sandbags. Together we pitched into the beaver dam and cleared it in five minutes. Again, Armando warned me to keep the beavers out.

"These damn willows," Armando said. "We'll never get rid of them. We're supposed to be able to walk the top of the ditch."

"It never used to be this way," Emilio said. "People let their goats eat the willows down. But nobody keeps goats anymore."

It was a perfect day for photos—the fields greening up, a pure azure sky behind snowy peaks. I tucked my camera in my fanny pack and shot two rolls over the course of the day, from early morning when we were still going strong, until late afternoon when we were beaten to our knees, dazed by heat and fatigue. I tried to capture the wrinkled brown faces of the old men, the shy young boys working steadily, whispering to each other, the patient, determined women. But there was no way to capture the musical Spanish phrases that flowed between the men as they chatted and teased. "*Mucho calor*," very hot, Esteven said, wiping his dripping forehead.

"*Cansado*," I'm tired, Ramon said, plopping his butt on the bank. He was tall with shoulder-length black hair. He offered his canteen. "*Aquí—agua*."

Estevan took a swig. "How come you're here? You don't own land."

"I'm a peón," Ramon said. "I'm working for the Zamoras. *Mucho trabajo, poco dinero*." Much work, little money. They both chuckled.

"I've been doing this for years," I said. "Wouldn't miss it."

Estevan turned his sharp, brown face to me. "I remember when you first started working with the crew. You had a big knife. The guys said, 'That woman is crazy. Stay away from her.'"

I slapped my gloves against my knee. "¡*Cuidado*!" Watch out.

At noon Karen and I trudged back to the house. I took a warm shower and changed my underwear. Karen and I ate salad at the outside table. Her face was bright red. "I don't know how you can stand it," she said. "That's it for me. I think I have heat stroke."

"You'd better go in and lie down." I hefted the shovel and went back to work.

Prickly Pear Cactus

*I*n the afternoon Sean suggested that he and I work in tandem, one raking the willows and dead leaves into piles, the other picking up the piles and tossing them onto the bank. We were schlepping a lot of debris—not just willows but dried green slime that looked like elephant snot.

I tried to curb my tendency to charge ahead of everyone else. Jack's wife Anna caught up to me. She was lean and brown, with long black hair fastened at the neck. Her hands were callused with digging in her garden, messing with horses, building fences. She clued me in on how to survive in Taos without a lot of money: "Plant a big garden and don't go anywhere." But at her end of the valley she had soil, not just rocks, sand, clay and caliche.

She and I raked ahead and Sean followed, picking up our piles. Contenta, our crew chief, whipped us along all day. In the old tradition she marked out with an adz twelve-foot sections, *las tareras*, for each of us to work individually. No one paid much attention to that—it was more productive to work side-by-side— but we needed more clippers and rakes. At one point she gave me the clunky adz to carry, like the burden of authority. I tried to trade it off, but no one else wanted it.

Now and then I'd climb to the top of the ditch to see where we were. "My God, this ditch is long." It wandered back and forth following the contours of the hillside and seems to run uphill before it crosses the highway.

As the sun fried our faces and necks, we took more frequent breaks, cowering in the shade of the bank. The men perched on the blades of their shovels. "It's not good to get stiff and damp from sitting on the ground," Ramon said. He took a swig of his water and offered me some. "What happened to Karen?"

I shrugged. "She thought she was going to faint." He laughed. I wiped my forehead. "You know how these Anglos are—they want to do this communal, close-to-the-earth stuff. They think it's romantic. And it is—for the first two hours." Another burst of laughter.

Freddie scratched his neck. "After that it's just outright abuse."

Twenty minutes later a photographer from *The Taos News* popped up to take pictures of us. Communal tradition. Even *National Geographic* got in on it a few years back.

As the sun sank toward Tres Piedras, Sean dragged the rake down the last eighth of a mile of the ditch. I paused to look up at Contenta who stood astride on the bank, hands on her hips. I gestured up and down the *acequia*. "Has our ditch ever been cleaned so thoroughly in the past ten years?"

She gave me a wilted smile. "No."

At the end of the day we returned to the culvert. Armando pulled up in his truck and called out the window, "Is that culvert clear? The water is coming."

Five or six men formed a "shit bucket brigade," passing buckets from hand to hand until they had cleared the pipe. They crawled out of the culvert and stood panting, waiting.

"Here they come," Freddie said.

Eloy and Marty were walking backward as fast as they could, tossing out tangled branches and debris with their shovels, barely keeping ahead of the churning tongue of water. Those who were still in the ditch scrambled up the steep bank as the muddy current flooded the culvert and gurgled out the other side, washing away everything foul and unwholesome.

Nobody spoke, but the same exultant smile lit each face as the living water glided by us, a mirror to the sky, swelling every crevice with moisture and possibility. Eloy nudged my arm and winked, "No *agua,* no *vida.*" No water, no life.

I grinned and nudged him back. "¡*Verdad!*" True.

The Paper Caper

*K*aren told me she had seen a job listing for a new paper called *The Taos County Eagle*. "They need a photographer/reporter."

Excited by the idea of working for a paper that was just starting up, I met briefly with Rafael Anuto from Peligro, a small town west of the Gorge. It was raining; we both showed up at the Peligro Grill in London Fog raincoats, like Spy and Counter-spy. He told me how much he loves newspapers, reads them front to back, "but I hate *The Taos News* because they're racist."

I handed him my résumé. He said he'd get back to me. The job is full time. Should I seriously consider it? I'd be out and about doing what I love to do—snooping, writing and taking pictures.

When I tried to phone the *Eagle*, I got a disconnect. Anuto called this morning to say he was in Taos, and could I meet him at Michael's Kitchen? I hurried in. After a few pleasantries, he said he was impressed with my résumé. "I see you're an environmentalist. How do you feel about the Pearlite Mine?"

"I think they've tried really hard to clean up their act. They do provide jobs."

He nodded. "What do you think is the most pressing problem locally, aside from zoning?"

"The economy. It's really hard to make a living here."

He seemed satisfied with that. He said the hours were flexible. "One week it might be sixty hours, the next week only ten. You might have to sit through long meetings. Writers keep their own hours. You know what it takes to get a story done."

"Will you supply a camera?"

"We're going to buy some. What do you suggest?"

"Nikon, definitely."

He said the paper would be a weekly, and they hoped to have the first issue out by May twenty-fifth. The job would be mainly going to county commission and school board meetings. Not as fascinating or creative as I had hoped. But he offered me four hundred a week. "I know your skills are worth more, but that's all we can afford."

I was going to ask for three hundred and fifty. He said they had funding for a year—then it would run out.

Suddenly I saw myself financially secure, helping Rachel get through school. I came away thinking I'd be crazy not to take it. That's twenty thousand a year. I've never made that much.

I dropped by Quick Copy and told Mara about my new job. She pulled a mouth. "Anuto was in here last week Xeroxing some legal documents. I know these guys. They're *politicos*," she said. "It's not a real job. They're just trying to influence the elections."

"You think?"

"The paper is probably being funded by Stanley Durango. He sold his land to the Pearlite Mine—he's former mayor of Peligro. I'm pretty sure he was involved in the bridge scam that was in the paper week after week about a year ago. They got county funding to build a bridge across the Rio Baca, but the materials disappeared, the deal fell apart, and one of the guys disappeared with the money."

"I hope it's not true."

She shook her head. "Stanley Durango is running for state

congress. Be careful. When Larry Ortega spoke out against the mine, someone burned down his outhouse."

"Well, dang! I'd hate to have my outhouse burned down, especially if I was in it."

Cholla

I went into *The Taos News* and leafed through a year of back issues. I found articles about the bridge, but there was no mention of Anuto or Durango. While I was there, I fell into a conversation with the editor of "Tempo." She said I did a good job with the art opening, and asked if I'd like to free-lance for "Tempo" once a month. I jumped at it. My second assignment is to interview Frank Waters, the revered author of *The Man Who Killed the Deer.* Whew!

The air was brilliant this morning, a few crickets chirping. The lilacs are scrumptious—fragrant. I drove out to Peligro this afternoon to attend a town council meeting. Stanley Durango was waiting for me in his office next door to the Cisterna Bar. (He owns the bar, too.) He was a big man, tall and wide, with a bald head, a bushy beard and red suspenders. He looked down at me with piercing green eyes and offered his hand. "Glad to have you aboard." He apologized for the state of the office. "We've ordered more desks and a couple of computers, but they haven't arrived yet."

"Do you have a camera I can use?"

He opened his desk drawer and handed me an old Pentax. "I don't know much about them. Is this one any good?"

I examined it. Everything seemed to be working. "May I try it?"

"Sure. Keep your receipts for the film and developing and we'll reimburse you."

I smiled. A writer-photographer's dream-come-true.

We drove over to the town hall in his long, low Bonnyville V-eight, gliding across the potholes like ducks flying over the lake. I felt conspicuous walking in with this huge man—I came up to his shoulder. He introduced me to the police chief and the clerks and told them I was here to cover the meeting for the *Eagle*. I was friendly, open. But I wondered what was on the agenda.

The meeting dragged on for three-and-a-half hours. They were trying to raise money to send a boy to Washington, D.C. with the high school mariachi band. I took a picture of him. The police chief gave him a hundred and fifty dollars. A man who wanted to start a brewery delivered a long presentation about how it would benefit the community. He said high school kids could raise hogs and feed them the leftover hops.

When he had finished, a long silence fell over the room. The chairman looked to Durango who indicated "no" with a slight swivel of his head. The chairman looked to the mayor who fumbled with his glasses, stood up and glanced around at the bored faces in the audience. He called for a vote. Without looking up from their agendas, all the councilmen murmured no.

Durango leaned over and whispered in my ear, "We don't need any more alcohol in our community. It's enough of a problem as it is."

I smelled booze and cigarettes on his breath. If he came on to me, I'd quit. I found myself wondering who the bad guys were. Or was it all just dirty politics?

They made Durango wait through the whole meeting to make his pitch for the *Eagle*. He asked permission to use an empty building at the end of town for his office. He introduced me. I stood up and smiled. He said they had employed six other staff members and ten writers. Why haven't I met them? How much do they pay them?

After some hemming and hawing, Mayor Maestas said the town planned to use that building for the handicapped lunch program.

Durango shrugged, "Well, let them have it. They're always getting left behind."

A fantasy flashed by me—what if this mountain of a man, under my benevolent influence, turned out to be a good guy after all? Uh-huh.

Hooray! Rachel is coming home for the summer. I'm cleaning her room, making space for her stuff in the back closet. She's driving down on Monday evening with her dad and his new girlfriend, Amy. I don't want to meet the woman.

I'm standing in front of the Cisterna Bar watching the bikers tool by like big, buzzing insects, cruising across the gorge to Peligro and back to Red River. It's the annual Red River Rendezvous, Memorial Day weekend. Durango, who has a dry sense of humor, says, "They drive up and down all night, back and forth, back and forth. They party, they piss everywhere. Then they get naked and throw up."

But he was smiling—bikers were partying by the six-pack at the Cisterna.

Anuto, Stanley and I met for coffee in the piss-stained bar and brainstormed ideas for the first issue of the paper. A couple of Forest Service guys were sitting nearby. I overheard them talk about sandbagging the river to prevent flooding. I suggested that for a story. Rafael said, "There'll be lots of room." After the meeting I drove up the highway and photographed places where the Red River was about to spill onto the highway.

On the way home I saw a wagon with mules grazing around it and pulled over. Camera in hand, I walked up to the camp. A man in a cowboy hat sat with two pieces of leather across his knees, sewing them together, while a white goat nuzzled his leg. I asked if I could take his picture. He glanced up at me, blue eyes smiling out of a lined but handsome face. "Sure."

He showed me his tooled leather belts, pouches, polished and graded leather beads. We chatted. The more I looked, the less I wanted to leave. Some customers pulled up. He asked for my phone number. I drove home grinning like Howdy Doody.

Not to say this had anything to do with Aaron and Amy arriving. I didn't even have time to vacuum. Suddenly they were here. Rachel snatched me off my feet and spun me around while I grunted and squealed. I hugged Aaron and shook hands with Amy, who is tall and slim, rather shy.

Aaron gave me a bottle of amaretto. I poured some for all of us. We sat outside for ten minutes, then Aaron showed Amy through the house. As soon as they had finished unloading Rachel's stuff, they fled. Out the kitchen window, I had one glimpse of Amy in the driveway with her arms around Aaron's neck, kissing. I felt a slight pang like the strap of one of my best high heels giving way, and it was over. I'm not hankering after the old life. I have my own life, and I'm excited about it. But I did entertain some fantasies about that cowboy who never called.

My interview with Frank Waters took place over the phone, long distance to Tucson where he wintered with his wife, Barbara. He said the cold was too hard on him now. He was very cordial, completely human. He is so in touch with the universe—I wish I had a chance to know him better.

I had a call today from a man named Bill Stuart, one of the reporters for the *Eagle*. He wanted to make sure we weren't working on the same story. So there really are other reporters.

——— ——— ———

Payday has come and gone. No check from Durango. I guess I'll have to take him to small claims court. It will be worth it. I called Rafael, who said he'd meet me at the post office at eight-thirty with a check. He wants me to cover the elections with him. If he shows up with a check for eight hundred, I'll do it. If not, I won't. If he shows with four hundred, I'll put it in the bank and wait for the rest before I do any more work.

I can't afford to volunteer. I wonder why I am still in this economic pinch while friends my age are redecorating their kitchens. I had this novel to write. Sure.

Eloy arrived and pulled the outhouse out of its hole by slinging a big chain around it and nudging it forward with the truck. I braced it underneath with a railroad tie. "Now fill up the hole with stones," he said.

"What can I pay you?"

"Make me a carrot cake."

——— ——— ———

I waited at the post office for over an hour for Rafael. Around one I called the employment office and asked how to file a complaint. They said they already had a complaint from a woman I've never met who is working in the production department of the *Eagle*. I saw the hope of some back-up testimony. I sat right down and wrote her a letter telling her what I intended to do: 1. Complain to the Labor Commission, 2. File in small claims court, 3. Complain to the Better Business Bureau and 4. Write a letter to *The Taos News*.

Around three, Rafael called. I said I wasn't going to cover the election unless I got paid for what I had already done. He said he'd pay me by Friday.

"No. Now."

He said he had had some unexpected expenses.

"You told me the paper was funded for a year."

"Things happen."

"You have to honor your contract with me."

"Document all the work you've done and I'll decide what you deserve to be paid."

"No. I'm working on a verbal contract of four hundred dollars a week, and right now you owe me twelve hundred."

His voice was tense. "Turn in all the work you've done, including the photos. And the camera."

"I'll deliver the camera when I get paid."

"Come to Peligro right now and I'll pay you."

"I'm busy. I'll send my daughter." I was trying to make my deadline on the Frank Waters story.

"No. You come. I want to talk to you."

"I'm working."

"Well, then . . ."

I called the Employment office and reported the conversation. They said it was okay to authorize someone else to go for me. "Write a letter naming the person and have them deliver the work. Say that you need the money and he has a legal obligation to pay you. And you'll give his camera back after you get paid. Have the letter notarized."

There was no time for that. I typed it up and paid Rachel five dollars to take it to Peligro. She delivered my letter to Bill Stuart; Rafael and Stanley had already left for the day.

I drove to town and turned in my story on Frank Waters. The editor of "Tempo" was pleased. She said my copy was "almost flawless."

Back home, I typed out three pages documenting my job with the *Eagle*, reconstructed from my journal and from memory, starting with the terms under which I was hired, ending with my plans to seek justice.

I had just finished when a shadow fluttered past my window. A red kite! Rachel was sitting on the roof, long hair flying in the evening light. I climbed up the ladder and sat beside her, grinning at the kite soaring on the summer wind. My drama seemed unreal.

Election night. I drove into town and headed for the courthouse with my documentation, the photos and my finished copy. Rafael and Stanley were sitting on a bench outside. I pretended not to see them, but I'm sure they saw me. I found a clerk, had the letter notarized, copied it and headed out the door. Stanley was gone; Rafael was flirting with a woman who sat beside him.

Something said, "Wait." The outside door was propped open and I stepped behind it. A few minutes later Durango strode in, dwarfing the people around him. I popped out from behind the door and handed him the packet. "What is it?" he asked, startled.

"Lots of things." I met his eyes. "Don't do this to me. I think you'll regret it. And so will I."

He took me aside, mumbled something about unexpected expenses—that he hadn't realized what Rafael had agreed to.

I poked out my chin. "You still have to honor the verbal agreement. If you want to, you can renegotiate it after you pay me."

"No."

"It doesn't have to end this way," I said. "I've enjoyed working for the paper. I put my heart into it. I paid for my phone calls, my film and developing."

"I'll pay you back."

"When?"

"Friday evening at seven at the office."

I wrote it down in my date book. He may not be there, but I will.

Showdown in Peligro. I invited my "family" to come along, Rachel as my witness and Karen as my bodyguard. I knew I wasn't going to get paid, but I had to go through the motions. It took us awhile to decide what to wear. I chose to go as Miss-Middle-Class in sandals, a white blouse and Rachel's royal blue cotton jumper. Rachel wore a green silk blouse, a black skirt and black stockings with seams. Karen fraggled her hair with hair spray and wore black lipstick, a transparent maroon silk blouse and a long black skirt with a slit in the side.

The parking lot was empty. Karen rapped hard on the door, but it was locked. After awhile Rafael came to the side door to let us in. Rachel and I sat in metal folding chairs while Karen paced. The first issue of the *Eagle* was stacked on the counter. I took one and started to read. Stanley Durango lost the race, but it was close. The paper didn't say by how much.

Rafael said Durango was in the shower, but he'd be here soon. Karen said in a hard voice, "Tell him to bring cash."

"What's the difference?" Rafael said.

Karen's eyes narrowed. "You know what the difference is. It's really hard on people, you know, having to chase the boss around to get paid."

Rafael fell back a step. "This is between Phaedra and me."

"Why don't you and Rachel go across the street and have coffee?" I said.

After they left, I asked Rafael what happened to the woman who worked in production. He said, "She's all taken care of. We advanced her money on her apartment. She took her breaks in the bar and drank on the job."

"You told me the paper was funded. What's the problem?"

"Mr. Durango's truck broke down and some of the finances had to be diverted to that. If he had won the election, we would have been fine."

I heard footsteps. Karen and Rachel returned. Then Durango's long shadow slid around the corner. He nodded to me and fiddled with some papers on his desk while Rafael answered the phone.

Durango said, "I'll write you a check and cash it for you."

Karen and Rachel hovered over me like two black Madonnas.

Durango complained that I had been working full time for *The Taos News.* I said that wasn't true, that I had put in my time for the *Eagle* and delivered the work he asked for. "The agreement between Rafael and me was clear."

"I didn't know about it."

"That's not my concern."

He sighed and stood up, reached into his back pocket, pulled out a wad of greenbacks and started counting one hundred dollar bills onto the table. I was dumbstruck.

"I didn't realize it was three weeks, not two," he mumbled. "I'll pay you eight hundred now. . . . "

"Okay."

Rafael made out a check for eight hundred. I signed it. Durango handed me the bills. I was about to go out and get the camera, but he said, "And I'll pay you the rest next week."

I stuffed the bills in my wallet, drew myself up and met his eyes. "I'll return the camera then."

Rafael gave me a weak smile. "Is this the daughter that's going to C.U.?"

"Yes."

"Why are you all dressed up?"

"We're going to Fiesta after this."

"Really?"

I laughed. "Sure."

As I turned to leave, he patted my shoulder. I think he was sincere.

We jumped in the car. I revved up the engine. "Let's hot foot it outta here before they change their minds."

All the way home, I kept looking back to see if they were after us, but all I saw was a cream-colored thunderhead billowing over the mountain. For hours I felt stunned. What to make of it? Eight hundred greenbacks. I felt as if I had stiffed the Mafia.

Negotiations

I applied for a FHA loan. They won't give me one because I don't have a good well, but there are other options. I called a lawyer about my property rights. She said if I took Aaron to court there was a fifty-fifty chance they'd award me half of the property. That's good to know. I don't want to fight Aaron, but I will if I have to. On the other hand, I don't want the sale of the land to drive us apart. With patience, I think we can work this out.

Aaron called in the evening and asked what I was up to. He sounded lonely, stressed out over work. He said he and Amy broke up two days ago. I said I was sorry, "But there's plenty of fish in the sea."

"That's what I figured."

He wants to come down and spend a few days with Rachel. I said sure. It might be fun.

Aaron is here. We took a walk by the river and talked. He told me his way of dealing with our separation was to jump into a love affair, but he wasn't ready to commit to anything, and she was. His main question was whether or not he and I were right to separate. I said yes, neither of us was able to grow anymore. He patted my shoulder. "I'm very relieved that you see it that way. Even though

I'm alone, I feel excited about all the possibilities."

"Good for you."

After all this struggle, are we becoming friends? Very strange. Or is it? The marriage worked for at least ten years. We never cheated, never lied to each other. At least we have that.

The Confluence of the Rio Hondo and the Rio Grande

We strolled across the bridge to the Cohns' and chatted with David at the long dining room table while Ellen fussed in the kitchen, fixing tea. I told them about my invasion of grasshoppers. "They're eating everything in sight. Rachel brought home some marigolds, which are supposed to repel insects, and now they're eating them, too. I sprayed with citronella and destroyed the lettuce and the pansies. Then Eloy came along with some netting, flung it over the garden and broke the heads off the marigolds."

Ellen said, "We don't seem to have a grasshopper problem."

David grinned. "Last summer I saw a horde of grasshoppers descending on my garden. Just before they reached it, a huge flock of magpies flew down and ate them. I've been fond of magpies ever since."

Miracles do happen.

Aaron asked David about his land deal. David tapped his pen on the table. "We're still negotiating the trade on our strip. I want to retain an acre on both sides of the river. I'll have my ashes scattered there."

Ellen said, "We like to picnic there."

Aaron offered the back hillside again. "Add that to the strip you already own on our side of the river and you'll have a big enough piece to build on. I could do terms, a down payment and a mortgage."

David lay down his pen. "We don't need it. We're struggling to get the kids through college."

Ellen turned to Aaron, hands on her hips. "You both have to cover your own asses."

Aaron sighed. "I'm tired of working so hard. I want to travel, to write."

David nodded. "I know what you mean."

Aaron and I paused on the bridge to watch the sheen of water slipping downstream. "It's over," he said.

"What?"

"Nobody wants that rocky hillside."

A cloud blew across the sun. I shivered.

He shoved his hands in his pockets. "Last week a man from Texas drove all the way up to Boulder to talk to me about buying our property. He offered me a hundred and fifty thousand. I've thought it over. He can have the whole thing for two hundred and twenty thousand. That would be a hundred and ten thousand to you. I don't think we should go any lower than that."

I bit my tongue and tasted the saltiness of my blood.

Aaron gave me a sidelong look. "Well, say something."

"I don't know what to say."

"I'm not giving up my power to sell the property. You can have input on the terms of the sale."

My face grew hot. "It's not like I never made any financial contributions to the family. I should have bought the house from you when Dad died. Instead, I just handed over my inheritance and let you spend it. Give me back the money my father left me when he died."

"Give me back the money my mother left me that I used to build the bathroom that you use every day."

I shut down in a black silence. My stomach churned. I wanted it over with.

He said, "Okay, let's sell the whole thing right now."

"Fine!"

He was silent a moment. "You don't consider the consequences of your words."

I turned to face him. "I went to see a lawyer."

He lost color; his eyes darted away. "I don't want this to turn into some awful . . ."

"Then wait."

"For what?"

Tears sprang into my eyes. "I don't know." I ran across the bridge and scrambled up the hill to the house. Rachel was standing in the doorway. "What's wrong?"

I waved toward Aaron. "Ask him!"

Aaron invited Rachel for a walk up the hill to find the spot where we buried his mother's ashes. Clouds blew in and a light rain swept the valley. I ran out to roll up my windows and sat for awhile in my old Toyota. Lightning flashed and rivulets of cold rain streaked the windshield. I gripped the wheel. At least this car was mine. I could always get in it and drive away. The Cohns were my last hope for hanging on to the house. I broke down and sobbed with my head on the steering wheel.

———— ———— ————

Rachel straggled in an hour later, pale and shaken. Dark tendrils of hair clung to her wet cheeks. I handed her a towel and set the kettle to boil. "It was dusk by the time we found Grandma's ashes," she said. "We just sat there in the rain. He was glugging a bottle of wine. I was crying. Mom, I just love him so much."

"Is he okay?"

"He wandered off by himself, half drunk. He was only wearing moccasins."

"I don't think he can get lost on his own land."

"But he could fall and hurt himself. Did you guys have a fight?"

"Did he tell you he was going to sell the property?"

She looked confused. "The house, too?"

"The whole thing."

She sank down on the couch and turned to me, her eyes dark with dismay. "We didn't talk about that."

I sat down beside her and we embraced. She clung to me. "I'm sorry, Mama."

"Me, too."

Dusk closed in. Roast chicken and veggies were getting cold on the table. I was about to grab a flashlight and go search for Aaron when he came bumbling in the door, wet and hungry, surprised that we had been worried about him.

———— ———— ————

At dawn I find myself standing on the petroglyph rock overlooking Hondo, weeping and praying for the strength to let go. Everything has come to a standstill, including my car, which wouldn't start this morning.

A pivotal pause. Moments that need to be honored before I rush into the next phase. Good-bye to my solitude, to the circle of blue mountains, to the murmur of the river. Get on with it. Let's have some resolution.

———— ———— ————

It rained last night. This morning I'm sitting at the outside table in brilliant sunlight. Steamy clouds are drifting from the dark sides of the mountains. The Apache plumes are fretted with silver drops of rain.

Aaron is still here. He and Rachel went out to a movie last night. I stayed home because I needed some time alone. I can feel a vast undercurrent sweeping through me, a swell rising from the bottom of the ocean. When I lit candles and danced in the living room I thought I felt an earthquake. I'm glad I did so much vigorous praying and focusing because today I feel solid and rooted in who I am—a woman who stands by herself.

After a long talk with Aaron, Rachel is mournful, but resolute. "Do what you have to do," she says. This will free up some money to help her and Brian through college and perhaps, at last, I can find time to write.

———— ———— ————

Aaron's last night here. I felt as if I was preparing the Last Supper. I made salad and cooked rice and salmon. Just as we were about to sit down to eat, the phone rang. It was David. "Is Aaron still there? I thought I saw his car in the driveway."

"Yes. Just a minute."

"Wait. This involves you, too. Our land trade fell through. Ellen and I have changed our minds. We'd like to buy your back hillside."

His words reverberated in my ear. "What?"

He laughed. "We'd like to buy the back hillside that borders our strip. That would give us enough land to build up there. We might want to sell this house when we retire."

I shook my head in disbelief. Aaron was watching my face. "What is it?" I handed him the phone.

Full Circle

*T*hat was seven years ago. Aaron sold the back half of the property to the Cohns and deeded over the house, the meadow and orchard to me. So here I am, pouring my energy into this old *casa*, which now owns me. To support it, I gave up my creative work for five years and took a full-time job as compositor and staff reporter for *The Taos News*, an important discipline and compost for another book.

But the job took too much out of me. When I broke my ankle I decided to take an early retirement. So here I am at home beside the Rio Hondo, thriving like a stubborn weed in the crack of the sidewalk, "living the life of a writer," freelancing for various publications including *The Taos News*, editing and teaching creative writing.

After the Hondo Fire, which blackened the mountainside from San Cristobal to Questa, I kept an eye on the tall weeds drying out in the orchard. One day I said to my old friend Glenda Gloss, "My pasture needs a horse."

She held up one finger. "I have a horse that needs a pasture."

I hired Eloy and his brother to put in the fence. A few days later Glenda delivered into my lush meadow a beautiful white

Arabian mare to graze all summer on grass up to her belly. She fits right into the neighborhood. In fact, I keep her in the Cohns' corral in bad weather. This plump little mare I call Krista is the first horse I've ever owned. Halfway between wild and tame, at first I thought she was too much for me. She startles at everything man-made and races up the canyon as if flying saucers were after her. I have learned a lot about courage and caution, but I still like galloping her bareback across the mesa.

I also enjoy viewing the countryside from the height of her back, and exploring trails I never knew were here. Last week I rode with Gillian who showed me a *torreón*, a stone turret on top of the mesa overlooking the Hondo valley. Archeologists say it dates back to 1820, that it was constructed and maintained by both the Spanish and local Indians to watch for raiders from the plains— Apache, Comanche and Cheyenne.

I have been traveling, too, enjoying islands in warm turquoise seas, diving the Great Barrier Reef, flying across Arctic tundra red as wine in the fall, gawking at grizzly bears and whales in Alaska. But I'm always glad to come home. Home is where I have composted my failures and reaped my choices. I'm still lonely sometimes, but Eloy brings me fresh trout and roses from his garden, and takes me fishing in the Rio Grande.

I am grateful to be rooted in this dramatic place with three cultures living together in conflict. The lively froth quickens my perception, hones the edges of reality and deepens the experience of living. The Indian and Spanish-speaking cultures, which have flourished here in the high mountain desert for centuries, have evolved their own survival skills. Most of the locals are tough and competent, and deserve to be heard.

In spite of their differences, the *gente* of Arroyo Hondo finally finished their heroic effort to restore *Nuestra Señora de los Dolores*. The wall around the church was completely mud plastered and the foundation reinforced with slabs of flagstone. Pat Montgomery painted an image of *Our Lady of the Sorrows* over the front doors.

Inside they pulled off the hard plaster and added a coat of soft yellow adobe mixed with white *tierra blanca* that sparkles with mica. The result is a luminous, peaceful interior. Carmen Velarde built the fireplace and Mary Cash Romero visited a museum in Colorado Springs where she copied the original altar screen. A full-sized reproduction now glows behind the altar.

Like Taos Pueblo, the church will now rely on community efforts to keep it in shape. And that's how it should be. "There are a lot more things that have been restored besides the building," Archie Trujillo said. "Almost everyone in the village either came to help at one time, or sent someone."

Lorenzo nodded. "This job couldn't have been done if it hadn't come from the heart."

"When you bond adobes together, you bond community, too," Larry Herrera said. He invited me to join them the next time I see them out there mudding.

———— ———— ————

I no longer feel like an outcast in my own community. Over the years I have won the grudging respect of some of the *gente*. I can see it in their eyes when they greet me at the post office and in the index-finger salutes from the steering wheel as we pass on the road. The sons of my *vecinos* bring me hay and *mayordomos* knock on my door to ask permission to cross my land with heavy equipment.

"Thanks for asking," I say.

Marcos nods with solemn dignity: "We will always ask. This is your land."

Like the birds, I am territorial, but it's not my land. I nurture the place and it nurtures me. My old friend Morgan Farley, who has been writing poetry for so many years, expresses exactly how I feel in her poem:

How to Own Land

Find a spot and sit there
until the grass begins to nose
between your thighs.
Track the creek through alder and scrub,
trade speech
for that cold sweet babble.
Gather sticks and spin them into fire,
Watch the smoke spiral into darkness.
Dream that the animals find you
They weave your hair into warm cloth
string your teeth on necklaces
wrap your skin soft around their feet

Wake to the silence of your scattered bones
Watch them whiten in the sun
When they have fallen to powder
and blown away
the land will be yours.

And Rachel's and Brian's. Aaron and the children still come home for the holidays. We've had some lively family reunions here, too. This year on Thanksgiving Aaron and I and Rachel and her partner William gathered at the dining room table for dinner. I lit the tall white candles and we held hands the way we always do before we gobble up any meal that takes longer than an hour to cook. "Thanks for coming down," I said.

Rachel squeezed my palm. "Thanks for being here." She turned to her dad. "Is there anything you want to say?"

He was looking handsome in a green corduroy shirt with a shaggy lock of hair falling across his forehead. He glanced at our faces, the candles, the hazy autumn sunlight slanting through the window. He nodded at me. "Thanks for holding onto the house. If it had been up to me, it would have been gone with the Schwinn."

I couldn't express how much that meant to me.

The birds flock to the nest, then fly away and I'm alone again. But I'm never really alone. In the fall I have bears lumbering through the orchard beating up on the apple trees; the deer grazing through the yard at dusk eating my daffodils; wild coyote cries to wake me in the middle of the winter night; and the song of the stones to lull me back to sleep. For better or worse, I am married heart and soul to the fierce and vibrant spirit of this land.

LaVergne, TN USA
14 September 2010
196988LV00003B/44/P

9 780865 345188